BOILING
MAD

BOILING
MAD

BEHIND THE LINES IN TEA PARTY AMERICA

Kate Zernike

St. Martin's Griffin
New York

www.stmartins.com

Designed by Meryl Sussman Levavi

The Library of Congress has cataloged the Henry Holt edition as follows:

Zernike, Kate.
    Boiling Mad : inside tea party America / Kate Zernike.—1st ed.
        p. cm.
    Includes index.
    ISBN 978-0-8050-9348-3
    1. Tea Party movement.   2. Tea Party Patriots   3. United States—
Politics and government—2009—   I. Title.
    JK2391.T43Z47 2010
    322.4'40973—dc22

                                                              2010025869

ISBN 978-0-312-61054-8 (trade paperback)

Originally published in hardcover format by Times Books,
an imprint of Henry Holt and Company

First St. Martin's Griffin Edition: October 2011

10 9 8 7 6 5 4 3 2 1

To my parents

Contents

PROLOGUE   1

ONE   *"This is America!"*   13

TWO   *"Hard work beats Daddy's money"*   33

THREE   *"Get off our backs, damn it!"*   49

FOUR   *"We look at the original, primary source"*   64

FIVE   *"Huzzah!"*   81

SIX   *"We've kind of changed the rules"*   99

SEVEN   *"It's a mission"*   120

EIGHT   *"We've been a little bit too nice"*   142

NINE   *"I have a message, a message from the Tea Party"*   160

EPILOGUE   183

AFTERWORD   195

APPENDIX   New York Times/CBS News Poll of *Tea Party Supporters*   211

ACKNOWLEDGMENTS   245

INDEX   249

BOILING
MAD

Prologue

Honestly, it was hard not to stop at the spectacle on Freedom Plaza in downtown Washington, where several thousand Americans had gathered to celebrate their anger on a perfect spring day. There was Representative Michele Bachmann, conservative darling and all Minnesota nice, cheerfully raging against "gangster government." "Two years from now, Barack Obama is a *one-term president!*" she taunted, the words echoing off the surrounding walls. There was the rapper performing a Tea Party anthem, the former *Saturday Night Live* star singing a song called "A Communist in the White House." It was easy just to scan the now-familiar signs—BARACK HUSSEIN HITLER, GO BACK TO KENYA—and conclude that you had seen all you needed to know.

But to truly understand the Tea Party, to understand how these protesters with goofy hats and "Don't Tread on Me" flags had become a political force powerful enough to confound a new administration and unhinge the Republican Party, you had to cross Pennsylvania Avenue and head down a steep escalator to a small auditorium inside the Ronald Reagan Building. Watch a crowd of a few hundred, dressed mostly in the sneakers-and-Dockers uniform of the typical older tourist, sitting rapt as a panel of conservative activists in their twenties explained how to take over the country. It was Tax Day 2010, and these Tea Partiers young and old were marking it with a seminar that blended modern managerial advice and leftist organizing tactics.

At the podium stood Brendan Steinhauser, a twenty-eight-year-old college football–loving Texan who had voted for Ron Paul in 2008 and could quote from the classics of Austrian economic theory but included among his heroes Bayard Rustin, the gay black civil rights leader who conceived the 1963 March on Washington most remembered for Martin Luther King Jr.'s "I Have a Dream" speech. The Tea Party movement had started out small, Steinhauser told the crowd, in the hundreds, but now, some polls showed that 25 percent of Americans supported it—remarkable growth in just one year. That percentage could reach fifty-one, he said, but he needed the help of the people in this room. "It's got to be a prime focus of what you do," he urged. "If you have twenty-five people there on your first monthly meeting, you should shoot for fifty, ask everyone to bring a friend. Try to set goals for yourself, set out where you want to be at the next meeting. Only if we focus on our numbers, check ourselves against other groups, are we going to get there."

There were two books every person in the room should read, Steinhauser said, repeating the titles twice, because most everyone was taking avid notes: *Dedication and Leadership* by Douglas Hyde and *The Tipping Point* by Malcolm Gladwell. The first, he explained, outlined how the Communist Party recruited in Great Britain, the second would help them understand the marketing of social phenomena—sneakers, but also ideas. "If you read those two books and apply the lessons and tactics learned in those," Steinhauser said, "I think you're really going to help yourself and really become a true community organizer."

"Uh-oh," someone said loudly. Others groaned.

"Don't reject that label! Embrace that label!" Steinhauser insisted. "True community organizers are what this movement is all made of. We don't like that term because now we have a Community Organizer-in-Chief who got his lessons from Saul Alinsky. I say, let's read Saul Alinsky, let's read *Rules for Radicals*, and let's use it against them!"

The crowd was his again. "Yeah!" people cheered, sustaining their applause.

"Do we need to do better to reach into new communities? Absolutely," Steinhauser continued, looking out at the sea of faces, almost all of them white. "I encourage all of you: recruit in the cities, the inner cities, in the suburbs, in the rural areas, in the barrios. It doesn't matter, wherever you live, wherever your neighbors are, get them involved and then go to some other part of town and get people involved who maybe you don't know. Maybe they're not in your social circle, they don't go to your church. You need to go and get to know these people and let them know that this is the kind of movement that welcomes everyone, that encourages everyone to participate. Only if we do that can we reach our goals." As the crowd cheered, he pressed on: don't give up on the apathetic, the people who voted for the Democrats. "Maybe they voted for Nancy Pelosi the first time, maybe they've had a little buyer's remorse," he said. "But don't write them off. Go out there, recruit people, bring new blood, new faces into the movement. Focus on that.

There is nothing more powerful that we can do for this movement than to go out there and recruit our friends and families
and strangers to become a part of it."

The contrast was striking: the panelists on stage were baby-
faced despite their suits and stylized stubble, while the people
in the audience were "seasoned," as one young panelist gently
put it—twice their age or more. When one young speaker
mentioned the importance of using social media like You-
Tube, an older woman with a drugstore disposable camera
and a flag brooch wrote down carefully "U2."

But this was how the movement had grown, this mashup
of young and old, abhorring the left but learning from it. It
was what made it so contradictory, and so combustible.

Loosely assembled and suspicious of anyone claiming to
be its leader, the Tea Party had allowed the rallies and the
signs to serve as the public face of the movement. But to stop
at what you saw there was to miss what the Tea Party was, and
how it had swiftly burrowed its way into American life and
wiped out the promise of a postpartisan politics that had accom-
panied the election of President Obama in 2008.

Its critics dismissed the Tea Party as "Astroturf," looking
like a grassroots movement but actually fake and manufactured
by big interest groups. Puppets of the Republican Party, they
said. Cranky old conservatives hung up on abortion and gay
marriage, now upset that a black man they didn't think was a
citizen was living in the White House. Who could take seriously
people who wore tricornered hats and inveighed against the
Communist threat twenty years after the fall of the Berlin Wall?
It was all a media creation. Just ignore them; they'll go away.

Certainly the Tea Party had been fertilized by well-connected
Washington groups like FreedomWorks, where Steinhauser
worked, and also by Glenn Beck, the newest star at the Fox News

Channel, who created his own brand of Tea Party by calling
for his fans to join "9/12 groups," which were to return the
country to the unity of purpose it felt in the days after the terror attacks of September 11, 2001. But even aside from these
well-connected supporters, the Tea Party was an authentic
popular movement, brought on by anger over the economy and
distrust of government—at all levels, and in both parties.

It certainly had its fringe elements: the birthers insisting
that President Obama was a Kenyan-born Muslim infiltrator,
the people carrying posters of Obama as a witch doctor, those
who insisted the federal government was going to sequester
its citizens in reeducation camps. As some Tea Partiers clam-
ored for states' rights, it was impossible to ignore the echo of
the southern segregationists from the 1950s and 1960s—little
surprise that the movement had failed to attract nonwhites in
proportion to their numbers in the country at large. Still, this
fringe did not define the Tea Party.

Nor could you explain it as simple partisan politics. While
most Tea Partiers were Republicans, they were fighting hand-
to-hand with the party establishment in places like Pennsylvania, Kentucky, Colorado, and Arizona, by mounting primary
challenges to establishment candidates once considered sure to
win, and seeking to take over the Republican Party in much
the way that Barack Obama's presidential campaign had won
the 2008 Democratic primaries, by sending supporters out to
become captains of their local voting precincts. By the spring
of 2010, many of the most active Tea Party organizers regarded
the rallies the way casual Protestants do church on Christmas
and Easter—the perfunctory appearances. They were too busy
operating as a kind of shadow party, hosting candidate forums
and meeting with officials—Democrats as well as Republicans—
who solicited their opinions and sought their blessing. They

were planning not just for the midterm elections that fall, but for the long term. And this wasn't just in off-the-grid Idaho or the Deep South. The Tea Party was everywhere—along the Eastern Seaboard, which Barry Goldwater said in the early 1960s he would saw off because there were no votes for conservatives there, and in swing districts where elections that determined control of Congress were often decided by a thousand or so votes and where presidential candidates fought every four years for the fickle middle ground.

To dismiss the grassroots popularity of the Tea Party movement was to discount the panic set off by the Great Recession, the growing anger about the staggering debt and the bailouts of carmakers, insurance companies, and the banks that had made it possible for people to buy houses they could not afford. It was to ignore the widespread and growing distrust not just of government, but of all the establishments Americans once trusted unquestioningly: doctors, banks, schools, the media. And it was to forget the opposition that had greeted attempts to overhaul the nation's health care system—or really, any ambitious progressive agenda since the 1930s—and the cycling of conservative insurgencies within the Republican Party. The Tea Party was not going away; in one form or another, it had been with us for a long time.

How big was it? In April 2010, fourteen months after the first Tea Party rallies, a *New York Times*/CBS News poll found that 18 percent of Americans defined themselves as "supporters" of the movement. Other polls put the proportion at 30 percent. Who were they? Almost uniformly white, they were disproportionately older than the general public, more likely to have a college or advanced degree, and more likely to describe themselves as fairly or very well off. This didn't make them affluent by many standards, but they were more prosperous

than the other Americans in the survey—less likely to have
annual family incomes under $50,000, and more likely to make
over $100,000. The Tea Party supporters were almost unani-
mously disapproving of the president and Congress, and they
were pessimistic about the economy and the direction of the
country by margins rarely if ever seen in previous polls. Given
a choice to describe themselves as "dissatisfied but not angry,"
53 percent opted for "angry"—angry about health care, about
government spending, about government "not representing
the people."

What did they want? While they took conservative positions on social issues like abortion and gay marriage, they did
not want to talk about them; they were more likely than ordinary Republicans to say that they wanted to focus on economic
issues.

Within the 18 percent who identified themselves as Tea
Party supporters was a smaller group, just 4 percent of the
American public, who attended the rallies and gave money to
Tea Party organizations. The demographic profile of these "Tea
Party activists" was almost identical to that of the larger group
of supporters. But they were distinctly angrier—three-quarters
of them defined themselves that way—more pessimistic about
the country's future, and more convinced that the bailouts
and the $787 billion economic stimulus package that Congress
had passed to stave off economic collapse had hurt rather than
helped.

Yet there were other dynamics no polls could reliably capture, things you had to observe up close, by watching the Tea
Partiers at their candidate forums, at the meetings where they
organized or the classes where they absorbed their view of the
Constitution, in their work as citizen lobbyists and fledgling
politicians.

While many observers emphasized the age of the Tea Partiers—a mere 3 percent of those who went to the rallies were younger than thirty, and only 17 percent were under the age of forty-five—the movement had been created and continued to be organized largely by young people like those on stage at the Reagan Building on Tax Day. These young Turks were well versed in the new social media that was changing political campaigns. And they provided the movement with an ideology, largely libertarian and marked by a purist and "originalist" view of the Constitution. Older people like those in the audience responded to the patriotism inherent in the talk of "liberty" and the pledge to be more faithful to the intentions of the Founding Fathers, and they grabbed onto the Constitution as the clear narrative to solve the country's complex problems. And it was they who formed the numbers that could swell street protests like the ones that first arrived in Washington in September 2009. Together, young and old alike, they became an impassioned community. Many described their Tea Party work—recruiting more people into the movement, teaching others about the Constitution—with near religious zeal. Some even quit their jobs to engage in it more fully.

In truth, the Tea Party had stepped into a void after the 2008 elections, when the right seemed to lack direction. Mainstream Republicans were licking their wounds after the loss to Barack Obama, and ideological conservatives were still stewing because the party had nominated Senator John McCain of Arizona, with his long history of compromises with liberals, as its standard-bearer. And as much as Obama had warned his supporters that he could not do alone what they had elected him to do, the grassroots that had worked so hard for his campaign never showed up when he needed their help pushing health care reform through Congress or rallying for the stimulus. They were too tired after a two-year campaign. They assumed his election was enough; their work was done.

But for all the Tea Party movement's energy and devotion, its shared sense of purpose, its May-to-September marriage of convenience might also weaken it. It depended on the blurring of ideological differences—a little like an older man ignoring that he had no music or cultural references in common with his young trophy wife. While the libertarians, typically younger, genuinely wanted to get rid of big government, and to phase out programs like Medicare and Social Security, the great majority of Tea Partiers believed those enormous government programs were worth the cost. Half benefited from them or lived with someone who did.

"That's a conundrum, isn't it?" said Jodine White, a sixty-two-year-old Tea Party supporter who lived in Rocklin, California, when she was asked in an interview after her participation in the *Times* poll how she reconciled wanting smaller government with being on Social Security, the biggest of the big government benefits. "I guess I want smaller government and my Social Security," she said. She had heart trouble, and was on her county health program. She would eventually need Medicare. "I guess I misspoke," she said. "I didn't look at it from the perspective from losing things I need. I think I've changed my mind."

She was hardly alone in her conflict. The contradictions of the movement reflected the confusion of a country that was more dependent than ever on government but at the same time more distrustful of it. Among the general public in the *Times* poll, only 20 percent said they could trust government most or all of the time. Similar numbers were reported by the Pew Research Center, which also found a rise in the number of Americans saying that government had a negative effect on their day-to-day life: in October 1997, 31 percent had agreed;

in March 2010, 43 percent did. Overwhelmingly, people saw elected officials as self-centered, irresponsible, and out of touch. Government wasn't helping average Americans, they believed; it was helping special interest groups at their expense. And this distrust wasn't just about government. It extended to banks, corporations, the news media, labor unions, the medical establishment.

Tea Partiers tended to believe that they had done all the right things in life: they had gotten married and had children, they went to church once a month or more, they paid their taxes (and most said they thought what they paid was fair, according to the *Times* poll). They had earned their place in the middle class, and they were out to protect what they saw as theirs. They distrusted people they regarded as elites, most notably the Obama administration, which they believed was embracing policies that favored the poor. They believed that too much had been made of the problems facing blacks. And above all, they had a visceral belief that government had taken control of their lives—and they wanted it back. Like many Americans, they had a strong faith in the autonomous individual. In the Pew survey, the public expressed its highest regard for small businesses and technology companies, the realm of the independent entrepreneur.

That explained why even though Tea Partiers told the *Times* poll that they were devoted watchers of Fox News, they also said that the information they trusted most of all came from others in the movement, not from the mainstream media. It also explained how they could be impervious to reports from the nonpartisan Congressional Budget Office, the closest thing the government has to a neutral arbiter, that the federal stimulus had cut taxes and created millions of jobs and that the health care legislation passed in 2010 would reduce the federal deficit.

Tom Grimes, a jovial sixty-five-year-old former stockbroker from South Bend, Indiana, had been laid off from his job and now called himself the "bus czar" for marshalling Tea Partiers to protests in Washington. He told how he had been communicating on Facebook with "some very progressive friends" who were arguing points made by Organizing for America, the grassroots organization that had grown out of the network of volunteers that had helped elect President Obama in 2008. "They sent out a letter, 'Five Things That the Other Side Is Saying That Are Totally Untrue,'" Grimes recalled. "I said, 'I don't care if they're untrue. It doesn't make any difference. The problem is, you guys are trying to sell this on facts. You can have all the facts, but if you don't trust the mind-set or the value system of the people involved, you can't even look at the facts any more.'"

Like the rally at Freedom Plaza, the Tea Party movement could be purely emotional. But then there were the people across the street in the Ronald Reagan Building making coolly rational arguments. Every time you thought you could put the movement in a box, you encountered something that didn't fit. The truth was, you had to understand all the parts to understand the whole. You had to understand the poll numbers and the larger trends, but you also had to see the varieties of Tea Party experience. You had to watch as people argued their case, not just on national television or with a homemade sign, but in the smaller encounters where they engaged with the movement.

It was easy, in some ways, to see how the Tea Party movement had burst out as the country grappled with the recession. The role of government was larger than ever, yet a bright future seemed anything but certain. But this was not some aberration of these difficult times. The Tea Party movement went to the heart of conflicts that had bedeviled Americans for more than two hundred years and reflected anxieties that Americans had been expressing for generations. If you opposed it, you could not just wish it gone. If you supported it, you had to consider its contradictions. You could not simply look away.

CHAPTER ONE

"This is America!"

The legend goes that it all started on the floor of the Chicago Mercantile Exchange on Thursday, February 19, 2009. There, a financial news commentator named Rick Santelli proclaimed on CNBC that the Obama administration's proposed mortgage assistance plan was "promoting bad behavior," rewarding "the losers" at the expense of people who had played by the rules. Surrounded by cheering commodities traders, Santelli invited like-minded capitalists to join him on the shores of Lake Michigan for a modern day Boston Tea Party in protest. "We're thinking of having a Chicago Tea Party in July," he ventured. Within days, it is said, millions of Americans sprang from their couches and desk chairs to take to the streets, and a movement was born. We the People, come to Take Back America.

It would be a wonderful creation story, if only it were that simple. In fact, the first Tea Party had already taken place three days earlier in Seattle, led by a twenty-nine-year-old woman named Keli Carender. If a lefty West Coast city was an unlikely cradle for conservative protest, Carender was an unlikely avatar of a movement that would come to derive most of its support from older white men. Half-Mexican, with a pierced nose, she taught basic math to adults on welfare and performed with an improv company on weekends.

But Carender's Tea Party protest, little more than a hundred people, showed almost perfectly in micro how the movement coalesced in its early months, combining resourcefulness and pluck with help from well-connected conservatives who were eager to spread the word.

Carender lived with her fiancé, Conor McNassar, in a neighborhood of Seattle with more ethnic grocers than coffee shops. They decorated their two-room apartment with Christmas lights and a whiteboard that ran almost the length of the living room. On it they sketched alternate furniture arrangements (mostly aimed at getting the television inherited from a friend out of the middle of the room) and to-do lists that offered the faintest hint of Carender's politics: "To buy: oven bulb, tires." "To read: *Mockingbird*, *Atlas Shrugged*." At once girlish and wonky, Carender pronounced articles of clothing she coveted "cute," and began an explication of her ideas about health care reform with, "On the one hand, I'm totally Randian . . ."

Her parents, who lived north of the city, were Democrats from Texas and New Mexico who met working on Capitol Hill in the 1970s. They left the party in the early 1990s because they felt it no longer welcomed those who, like them, oppose abortion. Her father had served in the military and worked as a lawyer before becoming a stay-at-home dad. Her mother was a claims examiner for the Washington State Department of Labor and brought home stories, Carender recalled, about how the department would go on a spending spree if there was any surplus at the end of the year, just to avoid having its budget scaled back the next year. "If that's not incentivizing waste," Carender said, "I don't know what is."

Outspoken about her conservatism in high school, Carender said she was more reserved when she got to Western Washington University—a "hippie school," by her definition— where it was assumed that everyone shared the same liberal worldview. "It was the first time I thought that what I believed was divisive or different," she said. "I was more interested in making friends." She studied math, and after graduation spent several months-long stints living and waiting tables in Australia, New Zealand, and Ireland. Then she went to Oxford University in England, where she earned a teaching certificate. She liked her job, she said, but it showed her up close how debilitating public assistance can be. A decade after welfare reform, her students bragged that it wasn't that hard to find ways around the requirement that they look for work.

She had started reading more about economics, mostly from the conservative perspective: in *National Review*, and in the writings of the libertarian economist Thomas Sowell, at Stanford's Hoover Institution. ("If I were president," she said, "He would be my economic adviser in a heartbeat.") In the months before the 2008 elections, she joined Young Republicans—"the only place to find conservatives in Seattle," she said, a city she called "a Mecca of radical liberalism." But like many conservatives, she had lost patience with the party for its role in the expansion of government programs and spending. Some went so far as to say that the Republicans had deserved to lose their congressional majorities in 2006; wasting time on wedge issues like gay marriage, the party had lost any claim on fiscal responsibility. Conservatives reviled President George W. Bush for expanding Medicare and increasing federal spending—turning the $236.2 billion budget surplus left him by Bill Clinton in 2001 into a $458.5 billion deficit by 2008 and nearly doubling the national debt, to $10.7 trillion. And they distrusted the party's 2008 nominee, John McCain, because he had reached across the aisle on campaign finance reform and on a bill that offered a path to citizenship for illegal immigrants. Carender, like many conservatives, hadn't thought much of any of the presidential contenders. "None of them seemed to understand what conservatives didn't like about Bush," she said, "that it was the spending." In the fall of 2008, as the bad mortgages and derivative securities that had presumed an unending rise in housing prices brought the economy tumbling down, the Bush administration responded with the Troubled Asset Relief Program, or TARP, to bail out endangered financial institutions. Then came the first bailout of the auto companies. To Carender, as for many conservatives, President Bush's explanation was laughable. "I've abandoned free-market principles to save the free-market system," he told CNN.

But she hardly welcomed President Barack Obama, with his promises of change. As the new administration began preparing a $787 billion economic stimulus bill in his first weeks in office, Carender said, "I started thinking, what are we getting ourselves into? It didn't make sense to me to be spending all this money when we don't have it. It seems more logical that we create an atmosphere where private industry can start to grow again and create jobs."

She tried calling her U.S. senators, Patty Murray and Maria Cantwell, both Democrats. "It was like a brick wall," she said. "I mean, I'd call every day and the mailboxes would be full. I'd call in the morning and it would be full. I'd call in the afternoon, it would be full. I understand: they had a lot of calls; it was just full. But I thought, maybe hire an extra person part-time to take down messages, or pay someone in the evening. That just seems like it's one of the most important things in a representative democracy, so it at least feels like you're getting through."

The recession was months away from becoming the deepest since World War II, and the administration was trying to act fast. Too fast, Carender thought.

"I felt like it was just running right over me and I didn't have any say in it at all," she said. "So I basically thought to myself, I have two courses. I can give up, go home and crawl into bed and be really depressed and just let it happen, or I can do something different and find a new avenue to get my voice out."

At her fiancé's suggestion, Carender started a blog, calling herself "Liberty Belle." McNassar, a quiet, dryly funny pension analyst, had voted for Obama, and he was patient with her complaints, but only to a point. ("He didn't mind hearing it," Carender said. "He just couldn't hear it all the time.") "My first thought is that we are not organized enough to complete the 'revolution' our country so desperately needs again," she began her first blog post. The Republicans, she argued, had failed to offer solutions to counter the "socialistic" programs of the Democrats. Conservatives, she proposed, should start a "solution revolution."

"I'm not saying alternative solutions that still mean big government, but rather solutions that real, everyday citizens could enact, without the government," she wrote. "We need something BOLD and DIFFERENT and REAL."

A week later, Carender decided bold had to begin with

protest. In previous years, she had watched the demonstrations in Seattle against the Iraq War and the World Trade Organization, and figured "if the antiwar people could do it, it can't be that hard."

She was also realistic about her ambitions. "I knew this wasn't going to stop anything, he's going to sign it, it's not going to stop them from voting for it," she recalled. "But at least I will feel as though I have tried as much as I can, that I've tried every option, and maybe I'll meet some people out of it and learn something."

She called the police about a permit, and they directed her to the parks department, which suggested having the protest in Westlake Park. And she came up with a name: "The Anti-Porkulus Protest," borrowing a term Rush Limbaugh had been using on his radio show. But she wasn't sure any protesters would come, beyond her parents and a few friends from Young Republicans. She called Michael Medved, the Seattle-based conservative radio host, thinking he would put out the word, but she couldn't get on the air. ("They put me on hold—'He's talking to a socialist right now, sorry.'") She scanned a list of economics professors who had signed a Cato Institute letter opposing the stimulus to see if any were from Washington State, but one lived too far east, and the other said he could not make it.

Still, he promised to spread the word, as did a former congressional candidate Carender had met at a convention-watching party the previous summer. She called Kirby Wilbur, a conservative local radio host with a drive-time talk show, who put in a plug. And she emailed Michelle Malkin, the conservative blogger and a Seattle native, who agreed to post something about the protest and to send over pulled pork from a place in Pioneer Square to feed the crowd.

The protest, held on Presidents' Day, drew mostly older people, along with a few in their twenties who had supported Ron Paul, the libertarian congressman from Texas, in his long-shot bid for the Republican presidential nomination the previous year.

The crowd was small enough that Carender did not need the microphone and amplifier that her parents had bought for the occasion. And there was plenty of leftover pork, which she took to a homeless shelter.

But remembering that Senator Barack Obama had collected email addresses on his book tour as he considered running for president, she took names and began to build a database for a group she christened Seattle Sons and Daughters of Liberty. Within the year, the list would grow to about two thousand addresses.

"People kept saying what's next, what's next?" she recalled. "We'd all been sitting around our dinner table with our families and just talking at each other. It was like this awakening. Everyone was just like, Oh my gosh, this feels so good to be doing something about how frustrated I am."

～

That you could find protest against the Obama administration's stimulus plan in a city that had voted more than two-to-one for the president just three months earlier hinted at the breadth of the anxiety about the economy and growing national debt. There had been other scattered demonstrations, too—Malkin had herself carved the roast pork at a protest in Denver the day after Carender's. And in Florida earlier that month, an out-of-work auto worker named Mary Rakovich had gathered a handful of people to hold protest signs outside a rally in Fort Myers where Governor Charlie Crist, a

Republican, was standing alongside President Obama to promote the stimulus bill.

What Rick Santelli did was give the discontent a name, and
a bit of imagery.

The administration's mortgage plan that so exercised Santelli proposed spending $75 billion to stimulate refinancing
for homeowners who had kept up their mortgage payments
but now owed more money to their lenders than their houses
were worth because of the steep decline in real-estate values.

Santelli, well-caffeinated on any day, seemed particularly
agitated on February 19, standing in his suit and tie on the
floor of the Mercantile Exchange and warning that the United
States could fast become Cuba.

"How about this, Mr. President and new administration,"
he offered, his voice raised, his vowels flat and Midwestern.
"Why don't you put up a website to have people vote on the
Internet as a referendum to see if we really want to subsidize
the losers' mortgages? Or would they like to at least buy cars,
buy a house that is in foreclosure—give it to people who
might have a chance to actually prosper down the road and
reward people that can carry the water instead of drink the
water?" At this, the handful of traders around him began to
cheer.

"This is America!" Santelli shouted, his arms waving at
the traders. "How many of you people want to pay for your
neighbor's mortgage that has an extra bathroom and can't
pay their bills? Raise their hand!"

"How about we all stop paying our mortgage?" the trader
standing next to him proposed. "It's a moral hazard."

"We're thinking of having a Chicago Tea Party in July,"
Santelli continued, the traders whistling now. "All you capital-

ists that want to show up to Lake Michigan, I'm gonna start organizing. . . . We're going to be dumping in some derivative securities."

"It's like mob rule," one of the studio hosts said.

"Hey, Rick," asked another, "Can you do that one more time, just to get the mob behind you again?"

"These guys are pretty straightforward," Santelli said, "and my guess is, a pretty good statistical cross section of America, the silent majority. And you know, they're pretty much of the notion that you can't buy your way into prosperity."

A commentator back in the studio congratulated him on his "new incarnation as a revolutionary leader." "Somebody needs one," Santelli replied. "I'll tell you what, if you read our Founding Fathers, people like Benjamin Franklin and Jefferson, what we're doing in this country now is making them roll over in their graves."

The next day, the president's press secretary, Robert Gibbs, criticized Santelli at a White House briefing. "I'm not entirely sure where Mr. Santelli lives, or in what house he lives," Gibbs said, "but the American people are struggling every day to meet their mortgage, stay in their job, pay their bills, to send their kids to school, and to hope that they don't get sick or that somebody they care for gets sick and sends them into bankruptcy. I think we left a few months ago the idea that what's good for a derivatives trader is good for Main Street."

But video of "the rant," as it became known, had already gone viral, with about a million people watching it on You-Tube over the next few days.

In Nashville, Michael Patrick Leahy had started getting

emails from young conservatives asking for his help planning Tea Parties. A fifty-three-year-old technology marketing consultant who had been a delegate for Mitt Romney at the 2008 Republican National Convention and had self-published books on Sarah Palin (flattering) and Barack Obama (not), Leahy believed that a technology gap explained what others called the enthusiasm gap between Democrats and Republicans. He argued that Obama had won the youth vote through social networking—YouTube, texting, Facebook. But the one technology the left did not dominate, he observed, was Twitter, the new sound bite–friendly service that allowed people to post messages of up to 140 characters to a retinue of self-selected followers. Shortly after Obama's victory in November, Leahy had started a list called Top Conservatives on Twitter, and invited people to begin coding relevant tweets with the hashtag #tcot. By February, there were about three thousand conservatives on his list, and now it was jumping about Santelli's Tea Party idea.

Leahy proposed a conference call for Friday evening, and about fifty people phoned in. One of the people who had asked for his help, J. P. Freire, a young editor at *The American Spectator*, announced to the call that he and some friends, young conservatives with jobs at think tanks, had already set a date and time for their protest—noon the following Friday in Washington. Good enough: everyone on the call agreed to synchronize their events across the country on that day. The group would hold conference calls every night for the next week to plan. And on Friday, February 27, they would count fifty-one events across the country, with thirty thousand people attending in all.

No one would be surprised to find big crowds turning out in traditionally conservative states like South Carolina, but there had also been Tea Parties in places you wouldn't expect—Hartford, Connecticut; Portland, Oregon; Boston, Massachusetts. If there was water nearby, people brought tea and dumped it. Everywhere, people brought flags and a sea of homemade signs:

STIMULATE BUSINESS, NOT GOVERNMENT.

YOUR MORTGAGE IS NOT MY PROBLEM.

THE GOVERNMENT HAS NO RIGHT TO TAKE OURS.

FREE MARKETS NOT FREELOADERS.

YOU CAN'T SPEND YOUR WAY OUT OF DEBT.

WE CAN'T AFFORD MORE CHANGE.

ENOUGH.

Something was in the air.

And on the air. The new street protesters had a powerful ally in Fox News, which had been searching out popular opposition to the stimulus bill. When Mary Rakovich protested in Fort Myers, Fox producers quickly got her to a local affiliate so she could be interviewed by satellite by Neil Cavuto in New York, even though her protest had, by her own count, consisted of herself, her husband, and one other person.

Sean Hannity replayed footage of Santelli's rant a few hours after it happened. The next day, Glenn Beck promoted the idea of tax revolts. And in the next several weeks, Fox would promote Tax Day Tea Parties—scheduled for April 15—in news programs and commercial spots. The network's anchors directed viewers to an online list of Tea Parties nationwide. Hannity attended the one in Atlanta. And Fox offered its own virtual Tax Day Tea Party for people who could not attend.

While Santelli's rant recalled the "I'm as mad as hell and

I'm not going to take this anymore" scene from the 1976 film *Network*, it was Fox's new star, Glenn Beck, who would soon assume the mantle of the film's rogue anchorman, Howard Beale. He railed against the Obama administration's "czars" and "Marxists." And on March 13, two weeks after the first nationwide protests, he dedicated an hour-long special to the birth of what he called "The 9/12 Project," encouraging people in advance to gather their friends at viewing parties.

The show opened with Beck narrating a round-the-world tour of global horrors: Islamic extremism, kidnappings on the Mexican border, soaring unemployment, high corporate taxes, Somali pirates. Then he harked back to September 12, 2001, the day after the terrorist attacks on New York and Washington, when "for a short time we really promised ourselves that we would focus on the things that were important. Friends, family, the eternal principles that allowed America to become the beacon for the world." The country, he said, needed to get back to that sense of purpose and unity.

He urged people to start 9/12 groups, based on "nine founding principles and twelve eternal values." "You can solve any problem if you just use values and principles," he said. The principles had a churchy overlay; "America is good," the first, was followed by "God is good, and he is the center of my life." The values were hard to disagree with: honesty, moderation, personal responsibility.

Beck promoted what would soon become Tea Party themes: that Democrats and Republicans alike were to blame. That free markets just needed room to work. And that it was the American people, not the elites in Washington, who knew how to confront the crisis.

"You know, many in Washington, left and right, want

to convince you that they're the solution," he said. "I happen to believe that them being the solution is the problem. The system has been perverted and it must be restored. Those who screwed up must be allowed to fail, those who broke the law must go to jail. Those who live by the rules must be left alone to rebuild the nation. The answers have never come from Washington."

Emotional and unpredictable—veteran television producers marveled at how a show so unstructured, with a blackboard as a chief prop, could produce such powerful television— Beck was mocked by liberals. But his just-between-us style, his openness about his struggles with addiction, and his sneering at elites resonated with a lot of Americans who felt they had no voice. It was to them that he appealed that night. "Let us find ourselves and our solutions together again," he said, and he began to weep, as he does frequently on his show. "I'm sorry," he said. "I just love my country, and I fear for it. And it seems like the voices of our leaders and special interests and the media, they're surrounding us, it sounds intimidating."

"But you know what," he said, his voice collected and cozily conspiratorial again, "pull away the curtain, you'll realize that there isn't anybody there, it's just a few people that are just pressing the buttons and their voices are actually really weak. The truth is, they don't surround us. We surround them. This is *our* country."

The 9/12 groups that started with the viewing parties that March night joined the growing loose confederation of Tea Party groups across the country. Technology made it easy to connect. Jenny Beth Martin, a thirty-eight-year-old former

Republican consultant in Georgia who was one of the conservatives on the original conference call that Michael Leahy
organized on Twitter, continued a once-a-week conference
call to plan Tax Day rallies. She already had what she called a
"mommy blog," posting mostly about her twins and how
she and her husband had struggled financially after his temp
business failed. By March, she had created a social networking site using a new technology called Ning, where budding
activists could communicate using their own individual
pages, find a local group or start their own, see calendars of
events, and get advice on how to hold a Tea Party (make your
signs brief, don't invite politicians to speak). Soon after Tax
Day, her website became the basis for a new organization, Tea
Party Patriots, with a growing email list. Eric Odom, one of
the young conservatives who had originally emailed Leahy,
maintained an email list of supporters on his Tax Day Tea
Party website. Supporters of Ron Paul's Campaign for Liberty, the group formed out of his 2008 bid for the presidency, began showing up at Tea Parties with RON PAUL 2012
signs. Paul's libertarian campaign had seemed destined to be
a footnote in the story of the 2008 election, but the Tea
Parties made it look as though he had simply been ahead of
his time.

   For these first organizers, the Tea Parties and the opposition to the new administration were a matter of ideology—
they talked about the importance of concepts like personal
property, liberty, or, like the commodities trader standing next
to Rick Santelli, moral hazard. A sign at a Denver Tea Party,
like many around the country, channeled the anti-collectivist
hero of Ayn Rand's novel *Atlas Shrugged*: THIS IS JOHN GALT
SPEAKING.

   But as the rallies grew over the next months, many of

the people who joined their ranks were acting on something more visceral—anger, fear. Most people were still having trouble making sense of what had happened with the economy in the first place—they may not have been able to understand the mechanics of collateralized debt obligations, but they saw clearly that the big banks had loaned money to people who wanted to buy houses they couldn't afford. Now executives at bailed-out firms like AIG were being rewarded with obscene bonuses? And the administration was going to overhaul health care, too?

In Lansdale, Pennsylvania, sixty-six-year-old Diana Reimer and her husband, Don, had been trying to sell their house so they could pay off some debt and move back to south Philadelphia, where they had grown up and could be close to their son. But they soon discovered that they owed more than their house was worth. "The Realtor told me, 'Oh, you'll only be about thirty thousand short,'" Diana recalled. "I said, 'Oh really?'" Don had lost his job, and she had gone back to work at Macy's, but even with ten years' experience at another department store, she wasn't earning as much as she had before. Rick Santelli might have called the Reimers "losers"; they were the people Obama's mortgage assistance plan would have helped. But Diana had not seen the rant. It was not until several weeks later that she saw something about the Tea Parties on Fox.

"I said, 'That's it,'" she recalled. To her, joining up wasn't a political statement. "It was a point of frustration," she said. "How can you get this frustration out and have your voice heard? They were doing something to be visible, rather than sitting at home and looking at the TV." She went online and signed up to become the Philadelphia coordinator for Tax Day Tea Party.

"It all started with the TARP, then Mr. Obama gets in and he's 'fundamentally changing this country,' and he's changing it, all right," she said. "The bailouts, the banks, AIG, and you see all the money these people are making and then all their bonuses, I mean, that's kind of ridiculous, who needs that much money? I just want to be able to pay our bills and stay afloat."

She and Don were on Social Security and Medicare, and received health benefits through the military's Tricare, because he had been in the Navy. She feared President Obama's health care plan would cut their benefits. "Where is he going to get this money?" she asked. "If the government wants to take away that privilege of Tricare for life, they can do that. If they want to take away my husband's retirement, they can do that. But people don't realize those things."

She had never been one to watch much television or read the newspapers. "This made us realize we had to be informed," she said. "We've never really done that. We've just sat back and trusted the government, trusted our elected officials. They were endorsed by the party and you trust them, and look the heck what happened. We're all at fault. We the American people, we're responsible, because we weren't paying attention."

Nearby, in Bucks County, a perennial battleground district in a perennial battleground state, Anastasia Przybylski was just the kind of voter the two parties haggle over. A thirty-five-year-old stay-at-home mother of three, she had voted for John McCain unenthusiastically in 2008. She had been a Democrat but had switched her registration to vote in local elections, where the critical choices were among Republicans. And she might have voted for Hillary Clinton, who had won the state's Democratic primary, had she been on the ballot in November.

Przybylski's worries about the economy had been mounting for months, beginning with high gasoline prices in the summer of 2008, moving on to TARP and the first bailout of the auto companies. After Obama's inauguration, she said, she wanted to believe that a new administration could make a difference. "I was hoping maybe they would be able to pull it together," she said. But after the stimulus bill passed in March, "I was just stressing about all this spending," she said.

"Where was the government going to get the money? What was the rush? I think it just alarmed America. The thing that stuck out was that no one was reading the bill, but there was this urgency. It was 'we've got to pass it now, we've got to pass it now.' I lost serious trust in the government at that point."

"Had they not passed all that so quickly," she said later, "it wouldn't have been the year that we've had with this Tea Party movement, honestly."

Przybylski had not been involved in politics, but about two years earlier she had met Mariann Davies, the daughter of Ecuadoran immigrants who had started a local anti-immigration group and was always forwarding Przybylski emails about political issues. After the Santelli rant Davies sent another email, proposing that they hold a roast-the-pork party. "Count me in," Przybylski replied.

They decided that if they were going to organize a Bucks County Tea Party, it had to be at the county's most storied site, Washington Crossing Historic Park, where George Washington launched the Christmas Night attack across the Delaware River that proved the resolve of the fledgling nation in 1776.

They put up a website, saying the date was to be determined. Every time she checked the website, Przybylski said, it seemed as if five hundred more people had viewed the page. She started losing weight, worrying about how she and Davies would pull off the event. "It was just the magnitude of it, being exposed, kind of coming out as a conservative," she said. "I've never done anything like that in my life."

With the growing national network of Tea Party groups planning rallies for Tax Day, Przybylski and Davies decided to hold theirs on Saturday, April 18.

In an exceptionally cold and rainy spring, it was a warm and bright day. About two thousand people filled the fields, bringing lawn chairs, tiny American flags, bold yellow banners with the "Don't Tread on Me" image from the Revolutionary War, and of course, the signs. One, ignoring all advice toward brevity, quoted Thomas Jefferson:

OUR FELLOW CITIZENS HAVE BEEN LED, HOODWINKED FROM THEIR PRINCIPLES BY A MOST EXTRAORDINARY COMBINATION OF CIRCUMSTANCES. BUT THE BAND IS REMOVED AND THEY NOW SEE FOR THEMSELVES.

Jennifer Turner Stefano happened onto the scene by accident. A former television reporter, she had given birth to her first child about a week after the 2008 election and had gone into new-mother cocoon. That Saturday, her first without visitors or rain, she told her husband that they were going to the park "if it kills me." As they got out of the car, she took in the flags, the signs, the country music blaring from the speakers.

"Jennifer," her husband insisted as she moved closer, "when you hear country music, you walk away from it, not toward it."

"Take the baby for a walk," she told him.

During the 2008 campaign, she had signed up for emails from MoveOn.org, the liberal activist group. She disagreed with everything MoveOn stood for, but she was impressed with how well it mobilized energy and voters, and wanted to learn from it. She had also called the local Republican Party, offering to volunteer—be a poll watcher, a precinct captain, anything—but she could barely get her calls returned.

She was struggling to find leaders she could embrace. She had voted for Democrats in the past, but she thought the party had been hijacked by liberals and had taken on an anti-American attitude. She was angry at President Bush for growing the deficit and letting foreign countries finance so much of the debt. She thought John McCain had lacked a plan for the economy, but on the other hand, Barack Obama's willingness to negotiate with Iran and Syria frightened her.

"No one was representing me—not the Republicans, not the Democrats," she said. "The Republicans gave away the country. Nobody cared about the middle class or the working class at all. Nobody cared about people like me, at all."

Now, in April 2009, as she surveyed the scene at Washington Crossing, "I just thought, where were these people?" She loved the speeches, the patriotism of the crowd, that the event had been organized by two women. "It was very motivated people, people a lot like me. They hadn't spent a lifetime being politicians; they didn't go to the Kennedy School of Government; they didn't work as a staffer on Capitol Hill. That's very refreshing."

While her husband was walking the baby, she later recalled, "I must have signed up for five hundred groups." She added her name to get emails from Ron Paul's campaign, to become a precinct captain, and for the Thomas Jefferson Club, a new local Tea Party.

"I don't think ten minutes before I walked to that park I knew what a Tea Party was," Stefano said. "At that moment, I was like, this is where I belong."

CHAPTER TWO

"Hard work beats Daddy's money"

FreedomWorks had been waiting for just this moment.

Since its founding in 1984, it had been trying to grow a grassroots movement that would make it more than just the well-connected Washington advocacy group it was, one that would produce a groundswell behind economic theories that rested lonely in academia. It had not had much success. Every April 15, FreedomWorks would hold protests outside post offices across the country—"Hate your taxes? Join us!"—but they rarely attracted more than a handful of people.

It had even proposed the idea of a modern-day Boston Tea Party—more than once. In 2002 it launched a website for the U.S. Tea Party: "Do you think our taxes are too high and our tax code too complicated? We do!" the site proclaimed, as "The Star-Spangled Banner" piped in the background. It mocked Tom Daschle, then the Democratic Senate majority leader, in a cartoon video game where a visitor to the site could click on boxes of tea to dump in the harbor while "Redcoat

Daschle" stood on the wharf demanding, "Gimme all your money!"

In 2003, the organization tried to raise its profile by bringing in Dick Armey as chairman. Armey, a former congressman from Texas and House majority leader, had been one of the leaders of the Republican takeover of Congress in 1994, and was a powerful voice in Washington in favor of lower taxes. But even he could not breathe life into the Tea Party metaphor. In 2007, he and the group's president, Matt Kibbe, wrote an op-ed article proposing the Boston Tea Party as a model of grassroots pressure on an overbearing central government. The men who dressed as Mohawks to dump the tea in Boston Harbor in 1773 had not simply shown up, they argued; Samuel Adams had tilled the ground for years, recruiting activists to his Sons of Liberty in the bars, shipyards, and shops of Boston, and enlisting wealthy businessmen like John Hancock in his cause. Presaging Tea Party tactics in the summer of 2009, they described how Adams packed town hall meetings with his supporters to drown out Tory voices and used each new British policy or tax as "an excuse to rally new recruits to the cause of American independence."

"Adams was the first American to recognize that 'it does not require a majority to prevail, but rather, an irate, tireless minority keen to set brush fires in people's minds,'" they wrote. But the op-ed lamented that conservative groups had "failed to effectively organize a cadre of vocal citizens willing and able to defend the principles of limited government."

"Clearly," Armey and Kibbe concluded, "we have a lot of work to do."

Clearly. FreedomWorks couldn't get the op-ed published

anywhere in 2007. Even Armey's spokesman thought the historical comparison "boring."

But all that changed in the first months of 2009. The mounting indignation about the stimulus bill gave Freedom-Works the grassroots ferment it had been seeking—an opportunity, as Armey and Kibbe had written of Sam Adams, "to channel outrage into action." FreedomWorks, in turn, gave people with inchoate anger something to do about it—organize. While many groups on the right moved to seize the Tea Party energy as it grew in the early months of 2009, it was Freedom-Works that moved first and most aggressively. And very quickly, the FreedomWorks ideology became the Tea Party ideology.

The group had been founded under the name Citizens for a Sound Economy, which was underwritten by the Koch family, the owners of a Kansas-based manufacturing and investment conglomerate that had supported many libertarian causes and think tanks like the Cato Institute. Citizens for a Sound Economy advocated a flat tax, and fought against ideas it considered big-government sins, like the Clinton administration's health care proposals in the 1990s and various proposals for a carbon tax to address global warming. Armey pitched the new name when he arrived, to echo one of "Armey's Axioms," the folksy aphorisms that reflected his North Dakota upbringing and his worldview. A former economics professor, Armey liked to lead crowds in cheers of "Freedom works! Freedom works!" as in, freedom for individuals and markets to prosper without government meddling. And so FreedomWorks it became.

At the group's headquarters on Pennsylvania Avenue in Washington, halfway between the Capitol and the White House, Dick Armey showed up mostly in the form of his official portrait, which hung in a conference room off the sparely furnished reception area. The real work of spreading the Tea Party brushfires was done by a small knot of about twenty take-no-prisoners young conservatives who worked there. In an elegant office building with an elaborately marbled lobby, their offices had the Red Bull-and-beer spirit of a fraternity or a political campaign. There were spent kegs on the balconies. Staff members boldly displayed emblems of the opposition: Max Pappas, the vice president for public policy, labored under a photograph of a smiling Franklin Delano Roosevelt signing the Social Security Act. A door bore a placard from an AFL-CIO rally for the Employee Free Choice Act and a Louis Vuitton advertisement featuring Mikhail Gorbachev (proof of capitalism's triumph over Communism). "We're like the Japanese," said Adam Brandon, FreedomWorks' press secretary and a Revolutionary War reenactor in his spare time. "We seize our enemies' flags."

They also loved a good gimmick. In 2008 they sent an intern dressed in a panda suit, via Starbucks and the Washington Metro, to the Capitol Hill home of Senator Christopher Dodd of Connecticut, carrying a giant mock check written out to him from Countrywide Financial after it was revealed that Dodd had refinanced his homes with VIP low-interest mortgages granted to friends of the company's president. The stunt was captured on video and posted to a website FreedomWorks created called AngryRenter.com. (Dodd, one of the Senate's most senior Democratic members, declined to run for reelection when his term was up in 2010, amid voter anger about the loans.)

Staff members liked to say they modeled themselves on Virgin Atlantic Airways or the Grateful Dead—Kibbe, the president and at forty-six the old man of the crew, was a follower

of the band, and the flowers and skeletons of Deadhead ico-
nography were displayed on the office walls. "They built this
whole community around the organization," Brandon said. "I
want people to think, when you join FreedomWorks, you're
joining a community—this is fun, man, we like each other."

They wanted the Tea Parties to be that way, too. But
Kibbe's goal above all was to create the MoveOn of the right.
And there was no doubting how serious FreedomWorks was
about organizing and spreading its ideas.

FreedomWorks was often described as a conservative organization, but strictly speaking it was libertarian. Like many
libertarians, the group was disinclined to talk about social
issues like abortion or gay marriage, because addressing them
required government intrusion on personal freedom. Instead,
FreedomWorks stuck to economic issues. It advocated a flat
tax, as Armey long had, with instructions simple enough to
fit on an index card, and personal retirement accounts instead
of Social Security. It opposed "card check," a proposal favored
by labor unions that would make it easier for them to organize, as well as a cap-and-trade energy policy, under which
companies would face a cap on their carbon emissions but
could buy or sell carbon credits depending on how much pollution they produced.

FreedomWorks had been founded on the theories of public choice and of the Austrian economic school, which had as
its stronghold George Mason University in nearby Arlington,
Virginia. Kibbe, wiry and intense, with angled sideburns and
architect glasses, had studied there before going on to stints
as an economist for the Republican National Committee and
the U.S. Chamber of Commerce. Austrian economics, built on

the work of economists such as Ludwig von Mises and Friedrich Hayek, argued that it was impossible to know all the influences on the economy and the variables of human behavior, so it was folly to rely on models and statistics to shape economic policy. Mainstream economists criticized this school of thought as unscientific and argued that it offered no real alternative to their models. But Austrian economists believed that the market, like water, finds its level, and thus should be left free from regulation, with consumers and price signals determining the flow of money. They opposed a central bank like the Federal Reserve and the redistribution of wealth through progressive taxation. Public choice theory argued that politicians will always act in their own self-interest, and therefore must be constrained by institutional rules. And on this front, FreedomWorks prized strict fidelity to the original words of the Constitution.

Fleshing out the FreedomWorks philosophy was the reading list Kibbe assigned every employee. Some of the books might be common at any corporate retreat: Malcolm Gladwell's *The Tipping Point* and *The Starfish and the Spider* by Ori Brafman and Rod A. Beckstrom, which describes the power of organizations that are built around an idea rather than a leader. Others were more political: Frederic Bastiat's *The Law*, a slim volume arguing against government spending on welfare, infrastructure, or public education ("eighty-eight pages of brilliance," Brendan Steinhauser, the group's director of campaigns, hailed it), and Douglas Hyde's *Dedication and Leadership*, lessons from the Communist Party on the power of indoctrination. And the reading list included three bibles of social activism: *Rules for Radicals* and *Reveille for Radicals* by Saul Alinsky, the founder of modern community organizing and a hero of the left, and *A Force More Powerful* by Peter Ackerman and Jack Duvall, about the history of nonviolent social movements in the twentieth century.

Staff members dropped references from these books into casual conversation. And they quoted any number of Armey's axioms; "Freedom works," of course, was a favorite, but they liked others, too: "Hard work beats Daddy's money" or "Government goes to those who show up." Sarah Palin had made *community organizer* a term of derision during the 2008 campaign by mocking Obama's experience as a young man in Chicago. But here, at the place responsible for mobilizing the Tea Party revolution, community organizing was religion. "You're a small group so you have to stick together," Brendan Steinhauser said. "There's something powerful about that. Creating this community through organization, that's what Obama understood so well."

Steinhauser, who hailed from Flatonia, Texas, population 1,377, was the main force driving the Tea Parties at FreedomWorks. Upbeat and idealistic, he had learned his trade by mobilizing young conservatives at the University of Texas in Austin, a liberal haven where bumper stickers urge residents to "Keep Austin Weird." He rallied his fellow conservatives to fight political correctness on campus, and after graduation he self-published a manual for young organizers on the right. "Today's generation of conservatives are still as bright and passionate as those of yesteryear, but we are indeed a new breed," he wrote. "The most striking difference of all is our propensity to fight. Our willingness to protest, counterprotest, and speak out for our cause is quite new to the movement."

He talked about "building the circle of power"—convincing a hundred people starts by convincing one, then two, then ten. And this was how he grew the Tea Party movement. It was a task made easier by technology—his first job for Freedom-Works, in the summer of 2005, had been to assemble the paper packets that the group used to mail out to its members to help them lobby their representatives in Congress. In early February 2009, he merely sent out an email to Freedom-Works' membership list saying it was time to take to the streets to protest the proposed stimulus package. He got a message back from Mary Rakovich in Florida saying that she and her husband were thinking of taking some protest signs to the rally in Fort Myers where Governor Crist was appearing with President Obama in favor of the stimulus.

Steinhauser had been leading activist training sessions in more than a dozen states in the previous months, focused on building local organizations, and Rakovich was fresh off a class. He called to press her to go, "even if you just take one friend." Afterward, he posted pictures of her three-person protest to the FreedomWorks Facebook page, encouraging other members to follow her lead.

On February 19, he and Adam Brandon caught Rick Santelli's rant live on television in the office. Within hours, they had set up a website called IAmWithRick.com, including a list of tips for how to hold a Tea Party protest: Create a Facebook page so that people can find you and the group can communicate. Write signs in BIG LETTERS. Call bloggers, talk radio hosts, and newspaper reporters to alert them. "Be loud, visible, happy, and engage the public," they wrote. "Wave your signs, make lots of noise and move around to get attention. If reporters interview you, give them some good sound bites for their stories. Stay on message and keep your answers short and coherent."

Take email addresses, the crib sheet advised, and send thank-yous to people who show up. "Now you have a list of people

in your community that can make the next protest huge," they
went on. "Encourage everyone to commit to bring at least
one friend to the next protest. Go find a friend in your neigh-
boring town or county and help them organize a protest there.
You and your people are now veterans and should be able to
keep the momentum going around your area." At the end,
Steinhauser offered his email address for questions or tips on
what to write on the signs.

Conservative bloggers linked to the memo. Steinhauser
then put up a Google map for people to find Tea Party loca-
tions, adding new ones as people emailed him. As other people
searched the web for "Tea Party" and found the map, they
asked him to post their events, too. When he and Brandon saw
that there were, say, four Tea Parties planned for Birmingham,
Alabama, they encouraged the organizers to combine their
efforts so that a single big crowd would attract more attention.

In his email in-box, Steinhauser set up a folder for each state,
saving messages from any potential member so he could connect them with the next person from that state who emailed
about starting a Tea Party. He mined for more members, and
encouraged local activists to do the same; in the early days,
before he was flooded with contacts, he would sometimes
reach out to people he had seen quoted in newspaper stories.
A year later, he would be keeping in touch with the network
mostly through one person from each state, who generally
knew what all the other groups there were doing. But he still
encouraged activists to read the letters to the editor in their
local newspapers to find people with like-minded opinions.

He began helping groups that formed after the first rallies
in February plan protests for Tax Day on April 15. When he
had thirty or so contacts for a particular state, he offered to

conduct a training session there, teaching rookie activists how to recruit and retain members, organize volunteers, and handle public relations. He advised the local organizers not to talk about President Obama, but to talk about issues instead. He also urged them to stay away from social issues. This was ideological guidance, reflecting FreedomWorks' focus. But it was also pragmatic. "It's going to split this movement, it's going to distract us," Steinhauser said. Besides, he added, "The debt is thirteen trillion dollars. Why would you focus on gay marriage when that's the real threat to freedom—the debt?"

He emphasized the importance of citizen lobbying, insisting that if you showed up on Capitol Hill with even three or four people in tow, your congressman would talk to you. (And think of what would happen if you could get thirty people!) "It does go back to community organizing, when Alinsky sends people in and says you've got to organize," he said. "It's about showing the elected officials that this group is active and that this group can affect public opinion in the district and that this group can get out the vote come election time. That's the circle of power. That's what I keep telling people when they say 'They're not listening.' When you get 51 percent of public opinion in your district, that's the goal."

From Bucks County, Anastasia Przybylski's connection to FreedomWorks was typical. She found Steinhauser's Tea Party map on a Google search, and as she planned her April 18 protest, she sent him a note asking him to add it to the map. A few months later, he suggested that he could do a training session for her and the members of other new groups in her area. She liked FreedomWorks' focus on fiscal discipline rather than the tired social issues, and believed it could help attract a wider range of supporters. She and other groups began crowding local meetings held by their congressman, Patrick Murphy, a Democrat. Soon, the local Republican Party was calling to ask to meet with her and other Tea Party leaders—and so was Murphy.

FreedomWorks worked particularly closely with Tea Party Patriots, which welcomed Tea Party groups and 9/12 groups under its umbrella to form a broad nationwide coalition with local affiliates—sometimes dozens of them—in every state. Anyone who Googled "Tea Party" would find that the Tea Party Patriots website was the first to pop up, with a link to locate a local Tea Party group, and a how-to for starting your own. Steinhauser was in near-daily contact with the group's national coordinators, people like Jenny Beth Martin and others who had started out leading local groups. The motto of Tea Party Patriots, "Fiscal Responsibility, Limited Government, and Free Markets," echoed FreedomWorks' mission. Local groups then picked up the mantra.

In all this, Dick Armey served as a kind of ambassador and recruiter-at-large, traveling the country to speak to Tea Party groups and to Republicans who were trying to understand them. The cliff of dark hair from his days in the House leadership had gone snowy white, but many conservatives, particularly older ones, remembered him as a leader from a time when the Republican Party was strong. And with his aw-shucks manner, he could make it sound as if the FreedomWorks philosophy—now the Tea Party philosophy—was the only reasonable hope of saving the country. People mobbed him at Tea Party events, wanting him to pose for photographs—for which he obligingly donned his Stetson—or sign autographs. They pulled out video cameras and cell phones to record even his casual remarks to a crowd.

In his House days, one of Armey's proudest accomplish-
ments had been working with Democrats who controlled the
chamber to create an independent commission that led to
the closure of nearly one hundred military installations that
had become obsolete. It had saved the taxpayers nearly $18
billion between 1989 and 2001, and an estimated $7 billion
in recurring costs each year since. He still held it up as the
model of bipartisanship. But in 2009, the mood of the country
had changed, and Armey seemed happy to foster the polariza-
tion. The Tea Party movement, he explained, "is really riding
now a crest of national fear. And the sum comment that you
hear is, 'These folks are going to ruin our country.' We've been
a great successful American experience, a blessing to all the
world because of private enterprise, individual liberty, and
our entrepreneurship, and these folks are going to destroy all
that."

Of the Tea Partiers, he said, "I don't think people understand how normal these folks are, and how diversified. You've
got evangelicals and libertarians walking hand-in-hand in the
cause of defense of individual liberties, against the encroach-
ments of big government in a myriad number of ways. You've
got Republicans, Democrats, independents. And yes, you have
some people also who are a little bit difficult to understand,
but for the most part, these folks are as normal as you and me.
It could be your mother, your father. I don't know how many
times I ran into somebody that is a perfectly normal person
that attends the PTA meetings, has their bridge club, and does
all the things you and I do that has sacrificed of their time and
expense to come to Washington or to go to the state capitol in
Michigan."

In 1994, when the Republican Revolution was coming
from within the party, Armey had been at the forefront, a

primary drafter of the Contract with America. Now, with the revolution charging from outside the establishment, he was once again at the head. If there was an irony in that, the people seeking his autograph did not seem to mind. Nor did they seem inclined to ask why he, as a member of the House leadership, had not been able to stop the expansion of big government and the runaway spending that Tea Partiers and FreedomWorks now raged against. For his part, Armey said that the Contract with America had been a good roadmap for keeping the deficit in check; the problem was that the Republicans in Congress "began drinking backslider's wine by the gallon."

Building the Tea Party movement, he said, would keep that from happening again. Describing himself as a "Goldwater boy," Armey called the Tea Party the fourth or fifth conservative wave since the 1960s. ("I can't always count," he said.) But as the first Internet wave, it would have more staying power. "I see these folks as pretty much the National Guard," he said. "They will go back to their day jobs, they will go back to their Little League and their bridge club. But they will have their activism at the ready, and they will stay in touch."

That comparison resonated with the young activists at FreedomWorks. "You go back to your Alinsky, go back to your Jefferson," Brendan Steinhauser said, "and there's this idea of perpetual revolution."

At the first Tea Party in Washington on February 27, 2009, Steinhauser had stood with a bullhorn and promised the crowd of about a hundred people, "This is only the beginning! This is a shot fired first that's going to be heard around the country."

Feeling momentum from that initial round of protests, he had begun thinking about organizing a march on Washington. He had been reading *A Force More Powerful* and appreciating the role played by Bayard Rustin, who with the labor leader A. Philip Randolph had first proposed a march on Washington in the 1940s, building the foundation of the civil rights movement for two decades before one happened in August 1963.

Kibbe pushed Steinhauser to focus on the groundwork. "Build, build, build," he said. "You've got to light the fires locally, then people are going to see." In March, Steinhauser registered for a permit that would allow FreedomWorks to hold a Tea Party march on Washington on Saturday, September 12. Just hours later, Glenn Beck hosted his special promoting the creation of 9/12 groups—providing a nice tie-in. "Which was pure coincidence," Steinhauser said, "even though no one is ever going to believe me."

But he kept building the fires. He created a FreedomWorks site on Ning, with a forum section where people could have discussions about, say, the cheapest plane fares or hotel rooms for the march on Washington.

And by summer, as Kibbe promised, the fires were spreading. The Tax Day rallies in April had crowds that FreedomWorks could have only dreamed of at their annual event just a year before. Then the local groups began organizing to confront their representatives about the proposed health care legislation during the congressional recess over the summer. Newly able to mobilize a bigger force of activists, FreedomWorks also prepared to take on a more aggressive role in elections. The group moved early to help conservative challengers (identifying them to Tea Party supporters as "champions of freedom") who were confronting establishment Republicans ("enemies of liberty") in primaries.

Kibbe likened it to the fifty-state strategy that Howard Dean had talked about as chairman of the Democratic National Committee leading up to the 2008 elections, building local organizations in states that Democrats once wrote off to the Republicans. "This is a legitimate fifty-state, every-congressional-district strategy," Kibbe said. "It gives our movement the opportunity to get on the offensive in places where a couple of years ago we couldn't." He marveled that there had been Tea Party events in liberal Brooklyn. In Hawaii, he met with a former Democrat who held Tea Party meetings in a union hall. "That," he said, "is amazing."

To the young staff at FreedomWorks, the goal was not just to learn from their opponents on the left but to beat them at their own game. "Obama's campaign did such a great job for Obama, but that's only got a shelf life for Obama," Steinhauser said. "This is about a set of ideas which people very much believe. This whole thing is baked in the Constitution and the Founding Fathers—that's a very powerful movement and an idea that's going to go on forever, whether it's Freedom-Works or Dick Armey or the Tea Party movement. It's bigger than all of that. It's about people believing in something they think is bigger."

In a few years, he argued, FreedomWorks wouldn't need to be doing rallies to call attention to its ideas; those ideas would pervade everyday conversations. "It's the little things, being at the bookstore and recommending a book, it's convincing a neighbor."

"My dream," he said, "is that we continue to connect the intellectual foundations of the movement to all these new people who kind of get this gut reaction that yes, America is this, and connect them to what's out there. My goal is to build long-term. You think about it, there wasn't a conservative movement before 1955. I want to look ahead at the next fifty years. That generation did that. I think our generation can take it to the next level."

CHAPTER THREE

"Get off our backs, damn it!"

After he appeared on morning television to talk about what was driving the anger in America, Donald Warren, a sociologist at the University of Michigan, received a letter from Anne Bowker, a woman in Tulsa, Oklahoma, sharing her thoughts on the subject.

"The government is almost afraid we will be self-reliant enough to solve our own problems without federal guidelines," she wrote.

> There is the perpetuation of the theory that the present time is almost impossible in which to live, and that we must change, change, change our whole life-styles and attitudes in order to survive into the future. Ahhh but "change" from what into what social order? And if change is to be necessary, just who will make the decisions? The people-planners or the people themselves? Since too many people-planners have this thinly

veiled contempt for the people, I am comforted in knowing they will get nowhere, though they do have our tax money to exploit for their own nefarious purposes.

It is the grassroots people themselves in whom I have a growing faith, once they are truthfully informed on the major issues. Americans are the greatest people in the world, with a marvelous sense of humor and genuine sense of joy in the here and now, and a faith in the future. From one individual to another individual the great silent majority is coming awake, and they will not be deliberately divided and collectivized into little warring groups. They are not isolated; quite the contrary, they need more privacy, more calm, peace, quiet and time to think. And most of all they need a sense of individual self-assurance that they can define and solve their problems with the help of God. But not with the "help" of government. Already they have just about helped us, and helped us to death. As the independent teen-agers say to their hovering, smothering parents, so we the people say to the social agencies: "Bug off. Get off our backs, damn it."

Bowker's letter could have been written by any Tea Partier holding a KEEP THE CHANGE sign at a rally—except it was written in February 1975, not in February 2009 as the Tea Party fires began to burn. And the frustrations Donald Warren was explaining were not those of Tea Partiers but of people he called "Middle American Radicals," the kind of grassroots activists who had supported the truckers' strike against high gas prices in 1974, the rights of West Virginia parents who were trying to ban textbooks they found offensive, and the protests against busing to integrate schools in Boston.

What explained the frustrations of the grassroots thirty-four years later? As the Tea Partiers began to make their case against big government in 2009, critics were particularly suspicious on one point above all: If these new grassroots protesters were so upset about deficits and the national debt, why hadn't they massed on the streets during the Bush administration as the numbers soared? The fact that they had not protested against George W. Bush seemed to the critics to prove that the Tea Partiers were motivated primarily by animus against Barack Obama and were therefore racists, their complaints about fiscal responsibility and big government just a thin disguise for their revulsion against the nation's first black president. TAKE OUR COUNTRY BACK, Tea Party signs proclaimed, to which critics asked, "Back *where*?" Presumably, to a time when a black man would not dare run for president.

Race certainly played some part in the opposition to Obama—or in creating a sense that he was Not One of Us. The fact that about 30 percent of the Tea Party supporters in the *New York Times*/CBS poll believed that Obama was not born in this country and therefore was not eligible to be president reflected that. So did the people who continued to insist, incorrectly, that he was a Muslim. You had to wonder, seeing the OBAMA'S PLAN = WHITE SLAVERY signs at rallies, whether anyone would have waved the same warning at any other Democratic president—Lyndon Johnson, say—promoting progressive causes like universal health insurance.

But if race was a factor for some Tea Partiers, a closer look at their complex motivations and historical antecedents suggested that it was not the driving force for a large number—and

possibly most—of them. To write off the movement as a back-
lash to the first black president was to isolate its sentiments as
a historical anomaly. As Anne Bowker's letter hinted, they
were anything but.

The Tea Party movement meant different things to different people—even those within the movement could not always
agree on what they wanted. But it borrowed its language and
its ideology from earlier conservative uprisings. The Tea Partiers' complaints were reminiscent of the accusations of "social-
ized medicine" that greeted the first attempts at national
health insurance in the 1940s. They evoked the libertarianism
embraced by many supporters of Barry Goldwater's presidential bid in 1964, and the tax revolts, textbook wars, and anti-
busing movements of the 1970s. Race was present in varying
degrees in many conservative insurgencies of the last fifty
years. But like the Tea Party, they were driven above all by antigovernment sentiment, as old as the nation itself. The American Revolution had been fought to oppose an overbearing
government, and for 230 years since then, Americans across
the political spectrum had asserted the rights of an Us who
had to take power back from Them. YOU HAVE AWAKENED A
SLEEPING GIANT, read one sign on Freedom Plaza on Tax Day
2010. You had to believe it had been more a nap than a deep
slumber, because those same sleeping giants had been coming
awake on conservative protest signs for most of the last half-
century.

In the most obvious way—the name—the protesters who first
took to the streets in February 2009 invited comparisons to
the colonists who stormed the ships on Griffin's Wharf in
Boston in December 1773 to protest the British taxes on tea.

The parallel worked as an accessible symbol of protest—from a young age, Americans learned about the Boston Tea Party as the quintessential act of rebellion, and forces on the left and right had been borrowing its imagery for years. (As Gordon Wood, the Pulitzer Prize–winning historian of the Revolutionary War, said, "Everyone wants to get right with the founders.") But "antitax" didn't best define the modern day Tea Partiers; in the *Times* poll, supporters could not agree whether they would prefer to cut taxes or reduce the deficit, and the overwhelming number thought that the main goal of the movement should be to reduce the size of government, not to cut taxes. By that measure, it made sense that they would oppose the Obama administration, because however much its agenda was intended to rescue the economy and extend health care coverage to the tens of millions who did not have it, it was by any definition an ambitious expansion of government regulation.

Some observers compared the Tea Partiers to the supporters of Ross Perot and his Reform Party in the 1990s; like the Tea Partiers, they were relatively well-off yet pessimistic about the country, and they had a devotion to their cause that at the margins could follow a conspiracy over a cliff. But the Tea Partiers had little interest in forming a third political party. And while Perot and his followers aimed to get special interests out of government, the Tea Partiers didn't care much about reform—they just wanted government out of their hair.

Though the Tea Partiers were often called populists, they were not populists in the traditional sense—that is, those who promoted social reforms and directed their anger at big banks and railroads. However much it might have made sense to blame Wall Street for the financial meltdown in 2008, the Tea Partiers were more inclined to blame Congress. Still, as the historian Michael Kazin argued in his 1995 book, *The Populist*

Persuasion, all populist movements, left and right, throughout American history, have shared a basic grammar and common themes. They championed "Americanism," the sense that the country is an ideology more than just a place on the map, one that treasures above all the will of the people. "This was the creed for which independence had been won and that all genuine patriots would fight to preserve," Kazin wrote. They valued a producer ethic, a belief that the people who did the real work—fought the wars, paid the taxes—were the true Americans. They believed that this justified them in being scornful of the undisciplined beneath them and the elites above them. And they viewed themselves as being on a crusade—saving the nation, restoring the "real" America.

This rubric described the People's Party fighting for the graduated income tax in the late nineteenth century and the Goldwater supporters arguing against it in the 1960s. And it well described the Tea Partiers proclaiming their superior patriotism and asserting that the Harvard Law School graduate in the White House was not going to use their tax money to pay for health insurance for people who did not have it. It was worth noting the declaration of Saul Alinsky, the father of modern community organizing and a hero of the left: "I love this goddamn country, and we're going to take it back."

Conservative populism, Kazin noted, was a contradiction in terms until the 1940s. Its rise was evident in the anti-Communist crusades of Senator Joseph McCarthy in the 1950s, but the right-wing grassroots truly began to gain mass strength in the early 1960s, in the Goldwater movement. The first years of the decade were "a time of effervescent liberalism," in the words of Lisa McGirr, in her 2001 book, *Suburban Warriors: The Origins of the New American Right*, which examined Orange County, California, as the hotbed of the sunbelt conservatism that gave rise to Barry Goldwater and Ronald Reagan. "While the student rebellions and the antiwar protests that would so strongly mark the decade had yet to heat up," McGirr noted, "the staid consensus of the 1950s had given way to a climate of change boosted by the energy, dynamism and youth of the Kennedy administration and a blossoming civil rights movement. It was a time when a deepening atmosphere for reform promised change on the horizon. It was a time, most of all, when the right felt bereft of power and influence." The censure of McCarthy and the death of Senator Robert Taft had left conservatives without a powerful spokesman in Washington during the latter half of the 1950s, and as the 1960s opened, Republicans were losing elections to a reinvigorated Democratic Party. "While, for liberals, the string of Democratic victories breathed new hope into the possibility of extending the liberal promise to all Americans through an expanded welfare state and civil rights," McGirr observed, "for conservatives, the Democratic resurgence heightened fears that the nation was on the road to 'collectivism.'"

Grassroots conservatives organized into groups, embraced the Constitution, pledged to repeal "the socialistic laws on our books," and entered local elections and the ranks of the Republican Party, "all in an urgent struggle to safeguard their particular vision of American freedom." They swelled the ranks of the John Birch Society, which was crusading against Communism and opposing racial integration in the South. Conservatives, McGirr wrote, "felt compelled to enlist in battle because of their sense of a widening chasm between the world of the New Deal liberal state and the values they found meaningful." They believed that the elites—President John F. Kennedy and his Harvard friends—were responsible for America's problems, that capitalism would take care of everything if the overgrown state would just go away, and that taxation violated property rights and amounted to government stealing.

The groups found their tribune in Senator Barry Goldwater of Arizona, who in his 1960 book, *The Conscience of a Conservative*, declared,

> I have little interest in streamlining government or in making it more efficient, for I mean to reduce its size. I do not undertake to promote welfare, for I propose to extend freedom. My aim is not to pass laws, but to repeal them. It is not to inaugurate new programs, but to cancel old ones that do violence to the Constitution, or that have failed their purpose, or that impose on the people an unwarranted financial burden. I will not attempt to discover whether legislation is "needed" before I have first determined whether it is constitutionally permissible. And if I should later be attacked for neglecting my constituents' "interests," I shall reply that I was informed that their main interest is liberty and that in that cause I am doing the very best I can.

Jump forward fifty years, and Tea Party activists were urging the identical aims. Rand Paul, the son of Ron Paul, was running for the U.S. Senate in Kentucky and had become the tribune of the Tea Party movement. Echoing Goldwater, he declared on the campaign trail that Congress should not be allowed to pass any legislation that was not explicitly authorized in the Constitution.

Race was not absent from the earlier conservative movements—hardly. In some instances, it was overt—the

Birchers argued that civil rights was a Communist plot, and joined other conservative groups in fighting for the repeal of antidiscrimination laws in housing. Goldwater opposed the Civil Rights Act of 1964 on libertarian principle, saying he opposed segregation but believed that forced integration violated all principles of liberty and free association.

Race was more subtle in conservative populist movements like the tax revolts that began in California and spread across the country in the late 1970s. With inflation causing a rise in property and income taxes even as the buying power of paychecks remained flat, citizen initiatives established laws capping taxes and cutting spending, particularly on social programs. "If you look at the tax revolt groups, a lot of it is, we're sick and tired of our tax money being used for 'them,'" said Bruce Schulman, a historian at Boston University and the author of *The Seventies: The Great Shift in American Culture, Society, and Politics.* "'Them' isn't always identified as blacks—these were middle class people who don't see themselves as racists, and they aren't—but it's clear that 'them' is racialized."

To understand the deeper social undercurrents, it's instructive to compare Donald Warren's studies of the "Middle American Radicals" (contained in his book *The Radical Center*) with the *Times* poll of Tea Partiers. You could think of Warren's radicals as the Tea Partiers of their day: They were mostly men, white, and older, and came from across the socioeconomic spectrum; they liked programs like Social Security but were angry at overreaching government. They tended to support the rights of parents who wanted to ban textbooks they found offensive, or who did not want their children to have to leave their neighborhood school for the cause of integration. In two surveys of just under two thousand people each in 1972 and in 1975, they expressed a deeply held belief that government was not working for them. Sixty percent, for example, agreed with the statement, "The rich give in to the demands of the poor, and the middle income people have to pay the bill." In the *Times* poll in 2010, 56 percent of Tea Party supporters said that the policies of the Obama administration favored the poor. In 1975, 53 percent of "Middle American Radicals" said that white people have "no responsibility" to "make up the wrongs done to blacks in the past." In 2010, 52 percent of Tea Party supporters said that "too much" had been made of the problems facing black people. Seventy-nine percent in the 1975 survey said that regarding welfare, "too many people think society owes them a living"; 73 percent in the *Times* poll said that providing government benefits to poor people encourages them to remain poor.

Answers on both surveys reflected a sense that the country had strayed on the moral and cultural issues of the day. The 1970s middle American radicals were more likely than other Americans in the survey to say that the generation gap was "very" or "somewhat" serious, more likely to favor teachers being allowed to spank children, far more likely to believe that "riots in cities are caused by agitators," and that "our main problem in Vietnam is the lack of patriotism in the United States." Tea Party supporters in 2010 were more likely than others polled to say that illegal immigration was a "very serious threat," that global warming would have no serious impact (15 percent volunteered that the problem did not even exist), that gay marriage should not be legally recognized, and that *Roe v. Wade*, the 1973 Supreme Court decision legalizing abortion, had been a bad thing.

As in the 1970s, economic insecurity intersected with cultural anxiety—a meat boycott in 1973 and the trucking strike galvanized anger about rising prices and stagnant paychecks.

What underlined the movements, then and now, was a sense among protesters that they were not respected and not listened to by the people in power. The parents demonstrating in West Virginia in the 1970s, many of them rural coal miners, believed that the elites choosing the textbooks and running the school board were mocking their religious views. EVEN HILLBILLIES HAVE CONSTITUTIONAL RIGHTS, one sign declared. Parents who opposed busing in Boston argued that it was unfair for the courts to force racial balance in city schools but not in suburban school districts that had even fewer black students. A sense of what Donald Warren termed "targeted alienation" made people believe that only they could be trusted to look out for their own best interests.

Mickey Edwards, a former Oklahoma congressman who supported Goldwater and served in the House Republican leadership in the early 1990s, said that for people he knew as a young person supporting Goldwater, the issue was not race or opposition to civil rights, it was smaller government. And the people he knew who were attending Tea Party rallies were not racists, and did not think, as he said, that Obama was "born on Mars." Their concerns were about health care and bailouts, but for the older supporters, he added, there was also a cultural dynamic at work. "They don't know how to work the computers; now everyone's doing texting," he said. "All of a sudden it wasn't just that people were gay, now they're getting married. All the things you grew up with, all the biases you had and believed were accurate, all the ways your daily life worked are being challenged. You don't have to be racist to look at: there's a black president, there's a woman speaker, it doesn't look the same."

Obama had always had trouble attracting support among older voters. Though he won a greater share of white voters in

2008 than Al Gore did in 2000 or John Kerry did in 2004, one of the few demographic groups he did not win were voters over sixty. And younger Tea Partiers, indeed, were less likely to see illegal immigration as a serious threat and more likely to support the rights of gays to marry. Obama had been elected on a promise of change, and change could be scary. "It's not a protest against a black man, it's a protest against change," Edwards said. "It's 'Leave us alone.'"

Decades of polling suggested that the numbers were probably stacked against a Democratic president to begin with—particularly one who took office in the middle of a sharp economic downturn. According to the Pew Research Center, trust in government is higher, historically, among members of the party that controls the White House, but Republicans are more trusting when a Republican is in the White House than Democrats are when a Democrat is in charge. And the low points of government trust were during the economic crises of the late 1970s and the early 1990s, and the one that began in 2008. Confidence in government rebounded when economic growth recovered. But the steepest drops in satisfaction with the state of the nation and trust in government were between the winter of 1991 and the fall of 1992. That year, a plurality of Americans chose "independent" as their political affiliation, and Ross Perot won 19 percent of the popular vote for president as a third-party candidate.

Had anything changed in 2009 and 2010? Certainly, the new forms of social media, and a well-established infrastructure for dissent, allowed the Tea Party to grow faster than any previous conservative movement. In 1978, the free-market economist Milton Friedman complained that "the market has no press agents who will trumpet its successes and gloss over its failures; the bureaucracy does." By the mid-1980s, as Bruce Schulman noted, "the private sphere could find dedicated publicists among progressive entrepreneurs and conservative ideologues, mall walkers, local governments, and health club members." By the first part of the twenty-first century, it had a sympathetic cable network in Fox. And while conservative groups of the 1960s and '70s relied on direct mail to get their message out, the Tea Partiers had email, Facebook, YouTube, Ning, and Twitter.

In an essay in the *New York Review of Books* published in May 2010, Mark Lilla, a Columbia University historian of intellectual movements, argued that the plummeting of trust in government and other institutions had coincided with a rise in the belief that individuals could do things better themselves. People didn't so much have a political grievance; they were simply tired of being told what to do. While historically, populist movements had seized political power for the people, the Tea Party movement wanted simply to neutralize government power. "It gives voice to those who feel they are being bullied," he wrote, "but this voice has only one Garbo-like thing to say: I want to be left alone." He called it "the libertarian mob," or the antipolitical Jacobins, drawing on the name of the French revolutionaries of the 1790s.

"The new Jacobins," Lilla wrote, "have two classic American traits that have grown much more pronounced in recent decades: blanket distrust of institutions and an astonishing— and unwarranted—confidence in the self. They are apocalyptic pessimists about public life and childlike optimists swaddled in self-esteem when it comes to their own powers."

Voters had become more likely to declare themselves independent and less likely to follow a political party's instructions.

They had learned to work around other institutions, too. The number of children being homeschooled had doubled in a decade. And with the proportion of people saying they had "hardly any" confidence in the medical establishment doubling since the early 1970s, more people were going on the Internet to diagnose themselves or were relying on unregulated herbal medicines. Parents who believed, against expert conclusions, that autism was caused by vaccines had pushed for laws in twenty-one states allowing exemptions to laws requiring school-children be vaccinated against highly contagious diseases.

The 2008 economic crash, Lilla argued, did more than shake people's confidence or devastate their finances: "It also broke through the moats we have been building around ourselves and our families, reminding us that certain problems require a collective response through political institutions." There was general agreement among policy makers that the government would have to intervene to prevent worldwide financial collapse or a true depression. "That, though, is not at all what people who distrusted elites, want to 'make up their own minds,' and have fantasies of self-sufficiency want to be told," he wrote.

Race could not explain the involvement of many Tea Partiers who expressed no hint of racist emotions, in the poll or in person. Anxiety about gay marriage or abortion could not explain why so many people who supported those rights, particularly young people, got involved. The distrust explained much more—it was pervasive—as did the anxiety about individuals not being able to set their own course. It was true of libertarians like Keli Carender who argued that health savings accounts and charity could be alternatives to government-run health care programs for the poor and elderly. It was true of the two women on Freedom Plaza on Tax Day, agitated that government could force you to wear a seatbelt but left it to women to "choose" whether to have an abortion. It was true of the elderly people who wanted their Medicare and Social Security but sloganeered about smaller government.

And it explained why so many saw a solution to their fears about the future in looking back, to the men who made the nation's first and boldest declaration of American independence.

CHAPTER FOUR

"We look at the original, primary source"

"If everyone could please stand, we're going to do a little exercise," Jared Taylor announced. "I'm going to teach you how to memorize the preamble to the Constitution using sign language."

Roughly a hundred people sitting in church rows in front of him, most well north of fifty years of age, stood up gamely as Taylor began: We (*hands to chest*) the people (*palms out*) of the United States (*fingers crossed*), in order to form (*hands molding a ball*) a more perfect union (*fingers curled together*), establish (*hands pressing down*) justice (*hands moving like scales*), insure (*right hand over left thumb*) domestic tranquility (*hands clasped to cheek, as in sleep*), provide (*hands out*) for the common defense (*hands fisted*), promote the general (*salute!*) welfare (*hand over heart*), and secure (*right hand grabs the air*) the blessings of liberty (*holding a torch*) to ourselves (*hands to chest*) and our posterity (*hands step upwards*), do ordain (*palms down*) and establish (*pressing toward the ground*) this Constitution (*unrolling a scroll*) for the United States (*fingers locked again*) of America (*arms waving, like an eagle in flight*).

Tom Grimes, sitting a couple of rows back, cheeks pink and delighted, called out, "This is going to turn into 'Y.M.C.A.' for Tea Party people! We're going to do it at all the weddings!"

It was a Saturday morning gathering of Michiana 9/12, a group that met in a low-ceilinged cement church on the farming outskirts of Elkhart, Indiana, the RV capital of the world and one of the high-unemployment cities that President Obama had visited in the winter of 2009 to sell his economic stimulus package. Taylor, an Arizona-based instructor with the National Center for Constitutional Studies, had flown in to teach a seven-hour seminar called "The Making of America." But as he helped his students fill in the blanks of the workbook that came with their ten-dollar admission fee, it was clear that most of the people here did not need sign language or anything else to memorize the preamble. Most of them, in fact, already knew several portions of the Constitution by heart.

It could be hard to define a Tea Party agenda; to some extent it depended on where you were. In the Northeast, groups mobilized against high taxes; in the Southwest, illegal immigration. Some Tea Partiers were clearer about what they didn't want than what they did. But the shared ideology— whether for young libertarians who came to the movement through Ron Paul or older 9/12ers who came to it through Glenn Beck—was the belief that a strict interpretation of the Constitution was the solution to government grown wild. "I'm not a Republican anymore," declared Susan Chilberg, a sixty-three-year-old woman who was in charge of legislative research for the Michiana group. "I'm a Constitutionalist."

This explained why Tea Partiers donned the hats of the minutemen who mustered in Lexington and Concord in 1775 and paraded the yellow "Don't Tread on Me" flags that Christopher Gadsden carried to the Second Continental Congress that same year. It explained the Revolutionary War reenactors giving the blessings at the start of Tea Party rallies, and the T-shirts the Tea Partiers wore quoting Thomas Paine, who said, "It is the duty of every patriot to protect his country from his government." They got their references wrong sometimes—a man in Grand Rapids, Michigan, wore a T-shirt attributing to Thomas Jefferson words that had actually been uttered by a well-known and more recent local politician, Gerald Ford: "A government big enough to give you everything you want is a government big enough to take from you everything you have." But the point was this: to the Tea Partiers, the Revolutionary War was more than a gimmick, and more than a metaphor. It was a frame of mind. They saw themselves the way they saw the founders, as liberty-loving people rebelling against a distant and increasingly overbearing government. By getting back to what the founders intended, they believed they could right what was wrong with the country. Where in the Constitution, they asked, does it say that the federal government was supposed to run banks? Or car companies? Where does it say that people have to purchase health insurance? Was it so much to ask that officials honor the document they swear an oath to uphold?

At the inaugural Bucks County Tea Party in April 2009, on the spot where George Washington launched his Christmas attack, a protester held a sign that suggested the gravity and the weariness of the historical embrace: HISTORY DOES REPEAT ITSELF: DECEMBER 25, 1776, APRIL 18, 2009. HERE WE ARE AGAIN. At a Tax Day rally in Washington, a man held a homemade poster with a picture of the Founding Fathers, and written underneath were the words MORE ANGRY WHITE GUYS. To the Tea Partiers, the Constitution made their movement more than a protest, and more than a partisan argument. There was no arguing with the Constitution. It was all there in black and white. As Dick Armey told one of his audiences: "If you don't understand the Constitution, I'll buy you a dictionary."

Tea Partiers handed out pocket versions of the Constitution like party favors at their events, and could quote from it, article and section. They attended seminars like the one in Elkhart, and supported candidates who called themselves "constitutional conservatives." Rand Paul, the U.S. Senate candidate in Kentucky who said that he would not vote for any legislation that was not explicitly authorized in the Constitution, made the case that Congress could balance the budget if it just got rid of all the programs that were unconstitutional—which meant a good deal of the legislation passed in the previous eighty years. The Contract from America—the brainchild of Ryan Hecker, a twenty-nine-year-old organizer of the Houston Tea Party Society, outlining what Tea Partiers wanted government to do—insisted that every new piece of legislation "identify the specific provision of the Constitution that gives Congress the power to do what the bill does." Another provision of the Contract from America would scrap the tax code and replace it with one no longer than 4,543 words—the length of the original, unamended Constitution. And as the Tea Party movement spread, so did a wave of state sovereignty laws across the country, declaring unconstitutional federal laws on gun control, or health insurance mandates. (Expressed colorfully on a sign at a rally in Washington: I LIVE IN VIRGINIA, STICK YOUR MANDATE UP MY . . . , over a red, white, and blue donkey.)

The Tea Partiers' view of the Constitution was commonly described as "originalism," a fidelity to the exact words of the document as they were written in 1787 that has adherents at major universities and, in Antonin Scalia and Clarence Thomas, on the U.S. Supreme Court. And some Tea Partiers' version of the Constitution sounded like just that. But many others were learning subjective interpretations of the Constitution that went beyond the primary source, and beyond what legal scholars or Americans would recognize—even using a dictionary—in reading the original document.

For more than two centuries, activists on either side of any number of issues have held up the Constitution to prove the righteousness of their cause. Civil rights demonstrators appealed to its provisions on equal protection; opponents pointed to its provisions on states' rights. But while conservatives and originalist legal scholars tended to argue against judges "legislating from the bench," the Tea Partiers were more focused on what they saw as abuses by Congress.

Above all, they emphasized that Congress had been granted only the powers enumerated explicitly in Article I, Section 8. That section of the Constitution mentions roughly twenty. They include the power to lay and collect taxes, to pay debts and provide for the common defense and general welfare of the United States. To borrow money. To regulate commerce "with foreign nations, and among the several States, and with the Indian Tribes." To establish rules on naturalization and bankruptcies, coin money and regulate its value. To punish counterfeiters, establish post offices and roads, promote "the Progress of Science and useful Arts," and to constitute tribunals "inferior to the Supreme Court." "To define and punish Piracies and Felonies committed on the high seas," to declare war, to maintain armies and a navy and a militia, to exercise legislation over the District of Columbia. And to sum up these powers, the framers declared that Congress had the power "to make all laws which shall be necessary and proper for carrying into execution the foregoing powers, and all other powers vested by this Constitution in the government of the United States, or in any department or officer thereof."

Whatever latitude this clause allows, the Tea Partiers believed that Congress had far exceeded it. They also believed that Congress had trampled the Tenth Amendment, which declared that "the powers not delegated to the United States by the Constitution, nor prohibited by it to the States, are reserved to the States respectively, or to the people." Nowhere in the Constitution, they argued, had Congress been given power to establish the Federal Reserve or any kind of central bank. It had no business establishing Social Security, or federal policy on education, energy, housing, labor—the list could go on, but they definitely believed that Congress had no role in regulating or mandating health care. Some resurrected decades-old arguments that the Sixteenth Amendment, which in 1913 allowed a progressive income tax, should not have been ratified because it violated the original Constitution—in the original, Congress could not levy a tax on the several states unless it was strictly "in proportion to the census or enumeration."

It wasn't that the Tea Partiers wanted no government, it was a question of which government would be in charge, and they believed it should be the states. The Independence Caucus, which provided Tea Party groups with lengthy questionnaires they could give to candidates to judge their faithfulness to the Constitution, argued that the Constitution did not give the federal government power to hold federal lands, and that these lands should be returned to the states. Other groups sought to overturn the Seventeenth Amendment, also ratified in 1913, which provided for the direct election of U.S. senators by the voters of each state—instead of having them selected by the state legislatures, as the Constitution had originally dictated. Giving up power at the ballot box might seem counter to the Tea Party's grassroots philosophy—indeed, the amendment was originally ratified after having been advocated by populists for decades. But the Tea Partiers saw its repeal as a way to return power to the state governments—and some also argued that if senators were less beholden directly to voters, they would not feel the need to bring home so many budget-busting pork-barrel projects.

Their view of the Constitution helped explain why the Tea Partiers were not so focused on the social issues that had been at the center of the conservative cause for four decades. They argued that the Constitution left it up to the states to decide how and whether to regulate matters like marriage or abortion. And in the case of gun rights, they believed the document provided blanket protection in the Second Amendment.

In the originalist view, and the Tea Party view, the perversion of the Constitution took off during the presidency of Franklin Delano Roosevelt. The legislation of the New Deal had aimed to relieve the problems of those hit hardest by the Great Depression and to prevent another one—among other things, the New Deal established a minimum wage and maximum hours, regulated banks, subsidized agriculture, and established Social Security. After the Supreme Court struck down much of the original legislation, arguing that the Constitution did not give the federal government such powers,

Roosevelt threatened to expand the size of the court from nine to fifteen justices so he could pack it with appointees friendlier to his agenda. He failed, but under the threat of that plan, Justice Owen J. Roberts reversed his position and upheld the constitutionality of a minimum wage law. That reversal—called "the switch in time that saved nine"—changed the tide of court rulings in favor of the New Deal. In some cases, such as the one upholding the Social Security Act, the court declared that the programs were justified under Congress' power to tax and spend. (The Social Security Administration attributes its survival to another tea party, the more traditional kind; according to the agency's official history, Frances Perkins, Roosevelt's secretary of labor, attended a tea at the home of Justice Harlan Fiske Stone where she confessed that the administration was not sure how it would justify the act. "The taxing power of the federal government, my dear," Stone is said to have replied. "The taxing power is sufficient for everything you want and need.")

The court's decisions also broadly expanded what Congress could do under the commerce clause, the provision in Article I, Section 8, that gave Congress the power to regulate interstate commerce. In their Constitution courses, Tea Partiers were taught that the most pernicious decision was *Wickard v. Filburn* in 1942. Roscoe Filburn, a farmer in Ohio, had been growing more wheat than he was allowed under limits the government had set up to control prices during the Depression. The court ruled that his extra crops, which he used to feed his chickens, reduced the amount of wheat he would have otherwise purchased on the market. And because wheat was traded nationally, his crops were affecting interstate commerce, and Congress could make laws regulating them.

In the decades since, the commerce clause has been the

basis for the bulk of legislation creating a strong federal state. Originalists argue that the clause was intended only to give power to regulate only the trade of goods between states, to prevent the states from erecting barriers to free trade. The most hard-core among them objected not merely to health care mandates but to the whole post–New Deal regulatory structure.

This kind of purist wanted to refight the two most important judicial wars in constitutional history, which had combined to move the country away from its founding-era view of the federal government. The first began with the Civil War and Reconstruction, when the states had become the tyrannical threat to individual liberty, and extended through the civil rights era of the 1960s. The Civil War and the three amendments passed in its aftermath—the Thirteenth, Fourteenth, and Fifteenth—established that when push came to shove, it was up to the federal government to protect the rights of citizens by imposing national values on dissenting states. It was through this revolution that the Constitution would come to acknowledge and protect the rights of blacks in the Jim Crow South. The second great constitutional revolution was instigated by the New Deal, when the Supreme Court's ultimate settlement gave the federal government expansive power over the national economy, which was broadly construed over time to encompass the environment, crime, education, and more.

These wars had been fought and won, and most people had moved on. To talk about states' rights in the way some Tea Partiers did was to pretend that the twentieth century and the latter half of the nineteenth century had never happened, that the country had not rejected this doctrine over and over. It was little wonder that people heard this echo of the slave era and decided that the movement had to be motivated by racism.

The Tea Partiers were not thinking in terms of stopping

blacks at the schoolhouse door; they just didn't want their taxes going to people who didn't have health care. The New Deal had come after years of populist agitation for programs like Social Security and enjoyed broad popular support during the Great Depression. Charles Wyzanski Jr., the government lawyer who won the cases that upheld Social Security, demurred when congratulated on his victory. "The cases were won not by Mr. Wyzanski," he said, "but either by Mr. Roosevelt or, if you prefer it, by Mr. Zeitgeist."

In the Great Recession, the zeitgeist was different.

⁓

Standing behind the Lucite pulpit at the church in Elkhart, Indiana, Jared Taylor began his course by making his students feel at one with the Founding Fathers. "If you were to describe the national mood," he asked the crowd, "what would you say?"

"Frustrated," replied one man.

"Fed up."

"Disgruntled."

"Angry."

"If George Washington came back," Taylor posed, "what would he say?"

"You foolish, lazy people," replied one man.

"Lock and load," offered another.

Taylor laughed, "I hear that!"

Modern historians, he told his students, put a "psychological spin" on these founders. "We look at the original primary source."

But his course, like many Tea Partiers across the country, in fact relied not on the original primary source but on what had become one of the most popular secondary sources on the Constitution: *The 5000 Year Leap* by W. Cleon Skousen. Published in 1981, it had vaulted onto bestseller lists in 2009 when Glenn Beck put it at the top of his reading list for the 9/12 groups. Beck gave out free copies to his studio audience, mentioned it frequently on air, and wrote a foreword to the book's thirtieth anniversary edition. The Michiana 9/12 group had been formed by the thirty-five-year-old owner of a local soft-pretzel chain on the night that Beck first called for 9/12 groups, and its members had read the book at Beck's suggestion. They then invited the National Center for Constitutional Studies, which Skousen had founded, to teach the seminar.

Skousen, who died at age ninety-two in 2006, was a Mormon and former Salt Lake City police chief who spent the 1960s writing and crusading against the Red Menace with a conspiracy theorist's zeal that made many conservatives shun him. He defended the John Birch Society against what he called a Communist attack, and later wrote denunciations of what he believed was a plot by bankers and groups like the Council on Foreign Relations to establish a One World Order. *The 5000 Year Leap* argued broadly that the Constitution had been inspired by religion, and that the framers had never intended the government to take taxes from one group so it could spend on another—as in programs like Medicare or Medicaid. It was a nation of charity, and charity, not government, should provide social welfare. The framers of the Constitution, Skousen wrote, were guided by twenty-eight fundamental beliefs that allowed the United States to make more progress in two hundred years than previous civilizations had made in five thousand—the nine principles that Beck wanted to guide his 9/12 groups had been boiled down from these. The founders' first principle, Skousen wrote, was a belief in Natural Law, or

God's law. The fourth: "Without religion, the government of a free people cannot be maintained." Thomas Jefferson had written of "a wall of separation of church and state," but *The 5000 Year Leap* argued that he intended this to apply only to the federal government—the founders, Skousen wrote, would have wanted the Bible to be taught in schools, and religious groups to be allowed to meet in public spaces.

The Constitution said little about how the nation's economy should be organized, but *The 5000 Year Leap* argued that the framers had very particular intentions. Skousen's seventh principle was "Equal rights, not equal things," which meant, in his explication, that "under no circumstance is the federal government to become involved in the public welfare. The founders felt it would corrupt the government and also the poor." Rather, people suffering misfortune should be protected by "the friendliness and charity of our countrymen." The founders intended the United States as a republic, he wrote; the popular perception of it as a "democracy" was the work of Socialists in the 1920s who intended to nationalize the nation's means of production and distribution.

Jared Taylor described Cleon Skousen to the group in Elkhart as a "great constitutional lawyer." The center, he said, had led eighty-seven similar seminars across the country in 2009, and in 2010 it was on track to teach twice that many, mostly to Tea Party groups. And he told his students that he wanted to "rewind the tape" to the origins of the Constitution. The founders had learned from the Crusades and the Bible, as well as the failures of the first settlers at Jamestown, which he described as the first attempt at "secular Communism." The settlers there were forced to put all the crops they grew into a central pool, he said, and therefore had no incentive to work hard, so did not produce enough to sustain the colony, which was nearly wiped out by death and disease.

This account of the Jamestown settlement, contained in Skousen's book, had become a cautionary tale at Tea Party gatherings; Dick Armey told audiences the same version. It glossed over the fact that the settlement had been established in an area plagued by mosquitoes and a lack of drinking water and had been repeatedly attacked by Indians. The settlers had not intended to grow crops but were focused on finding gold to send back to England and were to be fed by supply ships from London. The course also chose selectively from the words of the founders; it did not mention that Alexander Hamilton was a proponent of a central bank and had consistently argued that the Constitution's clause allowing Congress to make laws that were "necessary and proper" gave it implied powers well beyond those explicitly enumerated.

The Tea Party view of the Constitution often involved picking and choosing which clauses to ignore and which ones to emphasize. It ignored that modern-day Americans had little in common with the men who adopted the Constitution, who believed in slavery and could barely have imagined an industrial economy, much less the post-industrial, globalized economy of the twenty-first century—or railroads and telegraphs, much less airplanes and email. While some Tea Partiers focused on the income tax, they did not typically mention that under the most literal reading of the Constitution, the country could not have an air force.

Taylor did not mention that either. Instead, he focused on how the eighteenth-century anti-federalist George Mason had learned from English history that rights had to be specifically enumerated. In the workbook, Taylor walked his students

through the ways that "under a European centralist philosophy known as democratic socialism," Congress has given the
president "responsibilities never dreamed of by the founders,"
including for federal relief programs, Medicare and Medicaid,
the Department of Housing and Urban Development, the
Department of Education, the regulation of television and
radio broadcasting, the National Institutes of Health.

"The stuff listed here would have fallen to the states?" one
man asked.

Yes, Taylor replied.

And if Congress wanted the federal government to have
these responsibilities, how should it have declared so?

"By constitutional amendment," Taylor said.

"The proper role of government," he said, "is to protect
our rights."

"Yeah, right," someone said.

"Let them know," echoed Tom Grimes.

~

Tom Grimes had been to his first Tea Party in South Bend,
Indiana, in the summer of 2009, and almost immediately
started his website to arrange transportation for Tea Party
protesters to Washington. "BusCzar.com," as he called it, was
a play on how President Obama, in the Tea Party view, had
abused his constitutional powers to appoint White House
advisers to oversee jobs like health care reform and the auto
bailout without having such appointees subject to confirmation by the Senate.

The back of Grimes's teal Mercury Grand Marquis was
loaded with the literature of the movement. There was Glenn
Beck's bestselling *Common Sense* and *Arguing with Idiots*,
Bastiat's *The Law*, *The Federalist Papers*, *Liberty and Tyranny*

by the conservative radio host Mark Levin, *The 5000 Year Leap*, and *A Patriot's History of the United States*. "We don't just listen to Glenn Beck," Grimes said, "We take little threads of what he says and go out and do research."

The books helped reinforce the view that the Constitution had been violated, particularly by the New Deal, that government should get its hands off private property, and that true liberty required throwing off the shackles of an oppressive central power.

Grimes, loquacious and normally upbeat, had come to harbor deep suspicions of the Obama administration. "We're on an evolutionary path to national socialistic government," he said. "What happens in every Communist state is, increasingly the power and the oligarchy that was formed, they took out anybody that spoke out against them. We all believe that is a possibility for the ultimate conclusion of where we're headed right now. I don't expect that to happen, but once you head in that direction . . ." His voice trailed off.

Grimes had lost his job as a stockbroker in January 2009, and he complained that Obama's economic policies had aggravated the recession. "Keynesian economics was proven not to work well in the '30s," he said. "The only reason we pulled out of the Great Depression was the war. All the other countries in Europe had depressions around the same time, but theirs was called a depression, ours was called the Great Depression because FDR tried to spend his way out of the problem and it just doesn't work. You can't spend your way out of a recession. You have to cut taxes, cut expenses in the government and let the market go free and wild."

He had been on Medicare and Social Security since he was laid off. But he said he could do without those government programs. "If you quit giving people that stuff, they would figure out how to do it on their own," he said. "People would overcome it. It's the economic engine."

Tea Party organizing had become a full-time job, and his goal for 2010 was to elect more of what he called Reagan conservatives in the midterm elections. But after that, he said, he was planning to go into high schools to teach students about the first principles. "Catholics have catechism," he said. "We're going to have Constitution classes."

The class in Elkhart gave its participants the sense that they were at least doing something about what they saw as a federal government a few steps from tyranny. But their frustration ran deep.

As he discussed the Declaration of Independence, Taylor helped his students fill in blanks in the workbook outlining what he said was the founders' penalty for high treason. Traitors were "to be hanged from the gallows until unconscious," he read, "then cut down and revived, then disemboweled and beheaded, then cut into quarters, each quarter to be boiled in oil and the residue spread over the countryside so that the last resting place of the offender would be forever unnamed, unhonored, and unknown."

He paused to let the room ponder this.

"Is that like waterboarding?" one man finally joked.

"This is how much freedom meant to them," Taylor said.

As the class absorbed this, a man raised his hand with another question. We the people, he said, are now facing "progressives" whose agenda violates the Constitution. "When," he asked, "are they committing treason?"

"That's why we have the ballot box," Taylor said. "To hold politicians accountable."

The class had been sitting for nearly seven hours. As he wrapped up, Taylor suggested that the group continue the lessons in their monthly 9/12 meetings, taking one section of the textbook to discuss each session. But just learning about the Constitution, he said, was not enough. "I know the frustration out there," he said. They had to fight for candidates, help choose textbooks so young Americans would learn the proper version of history. They had to sit on school boards and city councils.

"There's a lot of momentum to restore constitutional government," he said. "But who's ready to run?"

CHAPTER FIVE

"Huzzah!"

Jeff McQueen stood outside an elevator at the Boston Park Plaza Hotel, waiting for a miracle.

The great-great-great-great-great-grandson of a Revolutionary War soldier, McQueen had created a "flag of the Second American Revolution"—Betsy Ross's circle of thirteen stars with a Roman numeral II in the middle—and it had become popular at Tea Party events across the country. Now the Tea Party was on the brink of the biggest event of its young life, helping to elect a Republican, Scott Brown, to a U.S. Senate seat that had been held by the nation's most storied Democratic dynasty for nearly a half century.

McQueen had driven seven hundred miles from his home in Michigan to be here. But security wouldn't let him into the victory party.

So he called his wife, who told him to pray for something to happen. And then, as he stood there silently beseeching, the elevator door opened. On the floor was a press pass to the party.

He called his wife back. "It worked!" he shouted into the

phone. He went upstairs with two hundred handheld flags
and waited until the crowd was shoulder to shoulder, spilling
out of the ballroom, to hand them out. As the jumbo televi-
sions announced Brown's once-unthinkable win, the throb-
bing crowd exploded into cheers, thrusting McQueen's stars
and stripes into the air above.

What's that flag? a cameraman asked him.

"It's the Tea Party flag!" McQueen cried out.

Everything worked for the Tea Party in Scott Brown's victory on January 19, 2010. It was a symbolic win, filling the
seat long held by the Senate's liberal lion, Ted Kennedy, with
a Republican who declared it "the people's seat." Brown's
election seemed certain to block the health care reform legislation the Tea Partiers so fervently opposed. It convinced people
who had dismissed the Tea Party as a passing political fad that
the grassroots rebellion would have real force in the midterm
elections the following fall. And it convinced the Tea Partiers
themselves that with enough determination, they could win
any seat they sought. Hard work beats Daddy's money.

But if it had come of age as a legitimate political force, the
Tea Party still struggled to control its fringes and its factions,
hinting at the problems of trying to be a "leaderless organization" that would be magnified in the months ahead. And as
much as the Tea Party was willing to work with Republicans
when they had the same goal—in this case, derailing the health
care legislation—the grassroots harbored deep distrust of the
party establishment. Lindsey Graham, the Republican senator
from South Carolina who had come under fire from Tea Party
groups for advocating the cap-and-trade of carbon emissions,
warned his colleagues to learn from the lesson of Martha
Coakley, Brown's Democratic opponent, who had been heavily
favored just a month before election day. "If you are a Repub-

lican in a red state," Graham told the *New York Times*, "don't think this can't happen to you."

⌇

In the eight months since the Tea Party's Tax Day rallies in April 2009, the brush fires that Samuel Adams spoke of setting in people's minds had spread to the streets and across the nation. Sometimes it was hard to remember that this was the same country where just months earlier, a record-setting crowd had converged in Washington on a bitter cold day to hail the inauguration of Barack Obama as the forty-fourth president of the United States.

As Congress began shaping an ambitious health care reform bill, conservatives fell into the same positions they had during the Democrats' last major effort, in 1993, invoking fears of health care rationing, long lines for treatment, and, in Sarah Palin's warning, "death panels" that would coldly calculate whether Grandma got to live or die. Tea Party groups had organized Independence Day rallies in July—what better holiday to celebrate the Second American Revolution?—then confronted senators and representatives at town hall meetings when they returned to their districts for summer recess in August.

A Tea Party Patriots organizer from Fairfield County, Connecticut—the land of Range Rovers and silver spoons— sent out a memo to other affiliates about "best practices" in challenging members of Congress at these town halls. "Use the Alinsky playbook of which the left is so fond: freeze it, attack it, personalize it, and polarize it," he wrote. He advised Tea Partiers to pack the hall, "watch for an opportunity to yell out and challenge the Rep's statements early. They need to leave the hall with some doubts about their agenda. The other objective is to illustrate for the balance of the audience that the national leadership is acting against our founders' principles which are on the other side of the debate—and show them that there are a lot of solid citizens in the district who oppose the socialist approach to the nation's challenges."

In seething confrontations, Tea Partiers accused lawmakers of promoting socialism, trampling on the Constitution, and trying to kill elderly people. "One day," a man in Lebanon, Pennsylvania, told Senator Arlen Specter, a moderate Republican who had switched to the Democratic Party that spring to avoid a conservative primary challenger, "God is going to stand before you, and he's going to judge you!"

The hostility played out on television and on YouTube, where 68,000 people viewed Keli Carender's town hall standoff with Representative Norm Dicks, the Democrat who represented her parents' district in Washington State. "If you believe that it is absolutely moral to take my money and give it to someone else based on their supposed needs," she told him, waving a twenty-dollar bill to the boos and cheers of the crowd, "then you come and take this twenty dollars and use it as a down payment on this health care plan."

Jenny Beth Martin, now the national co-coordinator of Tea Party Patriots, had continued her weekly conference calls, which now connected hundreds of local Tea Party leaders across the country. Michael Patrick Leahy had the Nationwide Tea Party Coalition. And more national groups sprung up. There was Tea Party Nation, which operated a kind of Facebook for Tea Partiers. The Tea Party Express, run by Republican consultants out of California, organized two three-week bus tours across the country in August and October, aboard a bus emblazoned "Just Vote Them Out!" A troupe of Tea Party entertainers rallied crowds with songs about the bailout and throwing the bums out in 2010. (One was to the tune of "New York, New York.") Oath Keepers, a newly formed group of military and law enforcement personnel who pledged not to enforce orders they found unconstitutional, dispatched its members to July 4 rallies with speeches declaring that they would not agree to orders to force Americans into detention camps—implying, of course, that this was about to happen. And a newly energized John Birch Society began setting up booths at Tea Party events and town halls. This led to accusations that the Tea Party movement was a cover for right-wing extremism, which in turn set off anger among the Tea Partiers, who said they were just peaceful citizens asserting their right to dissent.

In September, thousands of protesters descended on Washington, D.C., for the FreedomWorks 9/12 march. Officials declined to issue crowd counts, leaving it to organizers and their critics to fight about the size of the Tea Party's appeal. FreedomWorks initially said that the march had drawn one and a half million people—almost the size of the crowd at Obama's inauguration. Experts in crowd estimation who analyzed aerial pictures put the number at closer to 70,000, and the Washington Metro reported 87,000 additional riders for that Saturday. But by any of those counts, it was a significant demonstration. The costumes and signs in the crowds hinted at what had moved people to the streets: PULL THE PLUG ON OBAMA, NOT GRANDMA, read one sign. THANK YOU GLENN BECK! read another, held by a man in a tricornered hat. One woman carried a poster board with a picture of Martin Luther King next to one of Obama; written underneath were the words, HE HAD A DREAM, WE GOT A NIGHTMARE.

As the Tea Partiers gathered numbers and confidence, their fight with the Republican establishment broke out into the open. They were furious with Republican officials in Washington

for supporting moderate establishment candidates over conservative challengers: the National Republican Senatorial Committee had endorsed Arlen Specter over Pat Toomey in March,
only to have Specter defect to the Democrats the next month;
then that summer, the committee backed Charlie Crist, the
governor who had supported the stimulus bill, over Marco
Rubio, a young former speaker of the House, in the Republican
primary for the U.S. Senate in Florida.

Watching all this from a distance, it was easy to believe that
the Tea Party movement was just so much yelling and screaming about conservative purity. In this context, Scott Brown's
victory seemed to come out of the cold blue January sky. In
fact, the Tea Partiers had been laying the groundwork all along.

The Tea Party came to the Brown race with a fierce determination honed in losing its first electoral effort two months
earlier.

President Obama's appointment of the Republican congressman John McHugh as secretary of the army had prompted
the special election for his seat, in New York's Twenty-third
District. A vast, largely rural area upstate, it had not elected a
Democrat to Congress in nearly 150 years. But Obama had
won the district with 52 percent of the vote in 2008, and his
party was hoping for an upset. For their part, Republican leaders were looking for a candidate who would not need to spend
a lot of time building name recognition, and who would appeal
to voters' concerns about the crippled economy. Gathering at a
pizzeria in Potsdam to pick a nominee in July 2009, the heads
of the eleven Republican county committees in the district
chose Dede Scozzafava, a forty-nine-year-old moderate, a for-

mer small-town mayor and investment adviser who had served in the state legislature for a decade.

But the local Tea Party groups rallied behind a third-party candidate, Doug Hoffman, a fifty-six-year-old accountant who declared his message to be "smaller government, less taxes, fiscal responsibility, and not spending money you don't have." He proclaimed his mentor to be Glenn Beck. Scozzafava was a liberal on social issues—she supported abortion rights and gay marriage—but Hoffman argued that her biggest heresy was her support of the economic stimulus package and of the "card check" provision, which would have required employers to grant recognition to a labor union if a majority of workers signed cards saying they wanted one.

FreedomWorks and other conservative groups encouraged Tea Party activists to go to the district to campaign for Hoffman. Dick Armey went himself, and other conservatives like Sarah Palin and former Senator Fred Thompson endorsed Hoffman. The fervor ate away so much at Scozzafava's support that she abandoned the race three days before the election. She then threw her support to the Democrat, who won by two percentage points.

The Republicans who had supported Scozzafava argued that the loss proved that the party had to appeal to the middle— that ideologically rigid conservatives couldn't win. Tea Partiers laid the blame on the Republican establishment for denying primary voters the right to choose the nominee. They vowed to give "not one red cent," as one website put it, to the party committees soliciting money from Washington. "A lot of people are writing 'return to sender' on the envelopes," said Debbie Dooley, an antitax advocate in Gwinnett County, Georgia, who had become a national coordinator for Tea Party Patriots.

They vowed that next time they would be better organized. But they had not expected to get the chance so soon. And certainly not in Massachusetts.

In early December, FreedomWorks hosted a premiere for *Tea Party: The Documentary Film*, which chronicled the political awakening of Jenny Beth Martin and four other activists. Outside the showing at the Ronald Reagan Convention Center in Washington, organizers rolled out green Astroturf instead of a red carpet, to mock the way the way liberals had portrayed the Tea Party. As Matt Kibbe, the FreedomWorks president, walked the Astroturf with his wife, a man pulled him aside. He introduced himself as Bob Vorin and said he had driven all the way from Massachusetts because he didn't think anyone would listen unless he delivered the message in person. The Republicans could win Ted Kennedy's seat, he insisted. He laid out his analysis to Kibbe: It was a special election in the dead of January. The Christmas and New Year's season would make it hard to get voters' attention. Snow and apathy would keep turnout low. All these factors meant that if a devoted and energized campaign could mobilize its voters, it stood a good chance of winning. The primaries to choose the party candidates were not yet over, but the Democrats were assuming that they would win in a walk, in a state that had elected Ted Kennedy to that seat nine times. Meanwhile, there was a hard-working Republican candidate who was about to grab his party's nomination, a telegenic state senator named Scott Brown. (Vorin didn't say this, but as a young man Brown had been voted *Cosmopolitan* magazine's "Sexiest Man Alive.") And the Tea Party activists in Massachusetts were fired up.

Kibbe told Vorin to send Brendan Steinhauser an email, but the FreedomWorks president wasn't convinced. He always had two questions in judging whether to get involved in a race: Can your support make a difference? And can the candidate win? He wasn't sure the answer to either question in this case was yes.

But Kibbe also knew that if FreedomWorks could pull it off, it would be a huge victory. Aside from the symbolic beauty of replacing Kennedy, who had died in August, with a Republican, it would also provide the party its forty-first vote in the Senate, which it needed to block the health care reform bill that had passed the House of Representatives in November.

"The number-one driver was the health care bill. If we can get this—cap-and-trade, card check, the jobs bill, you can say goodbye," Steinhauser said. "It was about stopping the overall agenda."

Steinhauser called Matt Clemente, who had worked as an intern in the FreedomWorks office to help organize the 9/12 rally and had moved home to Massachusetts. Clemente reported that the state was papered with Brown signs, despite the fact that there were three times as many registered Democrats as Republicans. He had recently gone to a dinner meeting of the Worcester Tea Party to talk about the group's plans for 2010 and discovered four hundred people in attendance, with a line out the door.

With the opportunity now clear, FreedomWorks alerted "our best people," as Steinhauser called them, veterans of the upstate New York race. Alerts also went out on Tea Party websites and on mass emails; Tea Partiers arrived from Connecticut to campaign on weekends and evenings, while others came by bus from Philadelphia and North Carolina. Activists even came from as far away as Chicago and Colorado. They knocked on doors in the snow, they held signs, they drove people to the polls, they worked phone banks. Meanwhile, technology made it possible for Tea Partiers who couldn't travel to Massachusetts to make phone calls from their homes. They simply emailed their interest to the Brown campaign and received back a password to a website where they could click to call voters, reading from a script urging people to vote for Brown.

Tea Party money flowed in, too. By the last ten days of the campaign, with conservative bloggers now buzzing about the race, Brown began raising one million dollars a day, most of it in small donations and from out of state. He had expected to raise less than that amount for the entire campaign. The political action committee behind Tea Party Express spent more than $350,000 on television commercials and phone messages against Martha Coakley in the final weeks.

The Tea Party was hardly the only factor in Brown's win. Coakley helped, too. She campaigned lightly between winning the Democratic primary and the general election six weeks later. She also committed huge errors: She called Curt Schilling, who had been the hero of the Boston Red Sox' 2004 World Series championship—the team's first in eighty-six years—a New York Yankee fan. And in an interview with the *Boston Globe* she defended her strategy of relying on union chiefs, local officials, and other influence makers, saying, "As opposed to standing outside Fenway Park? In the cold? Shaking hands?"

Scott Brown, of course, was doing just that. Particularly in Massachusetts, where the only obsession bigger than politics is the Red Sox, voters swooned. He strummed all the right chords for the anti-incumbent mood. He drove around the state in his pickup truck and a Carhartt jacket, scenes replayed on his television commercials for anyone who didn't meet him in person. "It's not the Kennedys' seat and it's not the Demo-

crats' seat," he insisted in a debate, "it's the people's seat."
While Coakley had no public events on her campaign sched-
ule during the last week of December, Brown had six the day
after Christmas alone, and seven the next day. And his Tea
Party forces were finding little resistance. "You're not knocking
on doors for Scott Brown, are you?" one woman asked Diana
Reimer, who had come up from Philadelphia to canvass for
Brown. "You don't have to do that; we love Scott!"

The Democratic leadership in Washington had stoked
voters' anger about the health care legislation by engaging in
unseemly horse-trading to get the bill passed—securing the
final vote in the Senate from Ben Nelson of Nebraska by agreeing to pick up the entire cost of expanding Medicaid in his
state.

And Massachusetts' reputation as a solidly Democratic state
had been somewhat overstated; while its congressional dele-
gation had been all Democrats for several years, the voters of
the commonwealth had elected Republicans in four straight
gubernatorial contests before opting for a Democrat in 2006.
The bulk of Massachusetts voters were registered as neither
Republican nor Democrat, but as "unenrolled."

Still, there was no overstating the shot in the arm it was
for the Tea Party. The win showed that the movement was
capable of maturing, or at least of being practical. On the
issues, Brown was not exactly the Tea Party's kind of candidate.
As a state senator, he had voted for the Massachusetts health
care overhaul, widely considered a model for the national legislation the Tea Partiers were trying to block. But in the wake
of the upstate New York race, they had come to realize that
they did not always have to have a perfect candidate, as long as
the candidate served some other purpose. They wanted that
forty-first vote in the Senate, and they wanted to prove their

strength. "This is not so much about Scott Brown as it is about the idea that if we really collaborate as a mass movement, we can take any seat in the country," said Eric Odom, one of the original Tea Party organizers, who had gone to Boston to campaign for Brown.

Brown's victory speech in the ballroom at the Park Plaza caught the spirit of the time. "What I've heard again and again on the campaign trail is that our political leaders have grown aloof from the people, impatient with dissent, and comfortable in the back room making deals," he said. "They thought you were on board with all of their ambitions. They thought they owned your vote. They thought they couldn't lose. But tonight, you and you and you have set them straight."

"Across this country, we are united by basic convictions that need only to be clearly stated to win a majority," he said. "If anyone still doubts that, in the election season just beginning, let them look to Massachusetts."

⌒

As the National Tea Party Convention gathered in Nashville the first weekend of February, Scott Brown was not there. But his name was everywhere, cited as evidence of how the Tea Party could turn anger into power. "The earthquake" was how Mark Skoda, a fifty-five-year-old technology consultant who had been chosen as the convention spokesman, described Brown's victory. "We did it without pejoratives, we did it without name-calling, we did it without all the absurdity that one would suggest is the traditional anger of the moment. We grew up."

Tea Partiers were feeling bold.

Judson Phillips, the founder of Tea Party Nation and the convention's lead organizer, faced a phalanx of reporters that included representatives from CBS and Al Jazeera, and told them that he had invited the chairmen of the Republican and Democratic National Committees. He had not heard from the Democrat, Tim Kaine, and the Republican, Michael Steele, had expressed interest but then claimed scheduling conflicts, which Phillips called "really regrettable."

"Are they afraid of you?" asked a Radio France reporter, kneeling beside Phillips and holding a microphone to his face.

"They should be," Phillips declared.

Susan and Gil Harper had come from Cushing, Maine, the landscape of Andrew Wyeth, where she telecommuted to New York as a lawyer and he made furniture. Gil had told his wife that a ticket to the convention was the only thing he wanted for Christmas. When she had given it to him, she had said she would only come along wearing a hat and sunglasses, given the movement's rabid reputation. But now she was wearing neither.

"I think she's come out," Gil said.

Susan smiled back. "I'm not wearing a hat anymore," she said.

Six hundred people had gathered at the Opryland Hotel and Convention Center, a small planet unto itself, with several wings surrounding a terrarium-like public atrium where guests could take a riverboat tour, shop for overpriced children's sweatshirts or several brands of Tennessee hot sauce, and dine on any number of different cuisines. The delegates, as they called themselves, were a small fraction of the Tea Party movement, but a committed one—or at least, one willing to pay the $549 ticket price, plus hotel and travel. Another five hundred people had paid $349 to hear Sarah Palin, the keynote speaker, at a dinner Saturday night.

It was a far cry from the street protests. There were no signs—apart from a placard of Palin wearing her signature red jacket that someone had hung from one of the wrought-iron balconies overlooking the riverboat tours. From all appearances, the convention could have been an annual gathering of dentists or teachers. (Blissdom, a gathering of women bloggers, was next door in the conventions wing.) Delegates with name tags on lanyards browsed tables set up by vendors selling sterling silver tea bag pendants and Tea Party–branded coffee and tea. They alternated between PowerPoint presentations in ballrooms and an Irish pub across from a sports bar that would not have been out of place at an airport.

Skoda, who had recently begun putting his radio voice to use doing a Tea Party show on a station in Memphis, said he would personally remove anyone "looking pretty crazy." But it never came to that.

"This is a real working convention," he said.

People had come to organize. "The rallies were good for last year, because that's what we could do last year," said Phillips, who had kicked off his shoes while being wired for yet another television appearance. "This year we have to change things. We have got to win."

At a session on how to unite state Tea Party groups, a contingent from California was large enough that it split off into an adjacent ballroom to plot its campaign against Senator Barbara Boxer, a Democrat who had won her last election by twenty percentage points. Through the partition walls you could hear their communal cheer, borrowed from the Founding Fathers: "Huzzah! Huzzah! *HUZZAH!*"

At a panel discussion titled "Defeating Liberalism via the Primary Process," the room erupted in a standing ovation when Barbee Kinnison, a delegate from Nevada, stood up and declared her intention to unite Tea Party groups behind a candidate to defeat Senator Harry Reid, the Democratic majority leader. As the session ended a few moments later, people charged her to exchange cell phone numbers and pledges of support. "You need to come to California and help us defeat Nancy Pelosi!" one woman urged.

The crowd was largely middle-aged and older, which presented some problems. As Skoda taught a session on "Collaboration in the Cloud-Applied Technology" the discussion got hung up on basic questions, like how to do an effective Google search, buy a web domain, or send a mass email. (Recognizing the demographics of the movement, one activist leading a session about how to organize suggested holding Tea Party Tuesdays or Tea Party Thursdays because the alliteration would help older people remember the day better.)

But the bigger problem was that the Tea Party could not agree on what it was about. Speakers cautioned against getting involved in divisive social issues. But that admonition went out the window the first night, as Tom Tancredo, a former congressman from Colorado who ran for president unsuccessfully on an anti-immigration platform, gave the kickoff speech. He railed against "the cult of multiculturalism, aided by leftist liberals all over, who don't have the same ideas about America as we do." He blamed the country's current troubles on the lack of a civics literacy test as a requirement to vote. "People who couldn't even spell the word 'vote' or say it in English, put a committed socialist ideologue in the White House," he declared. "His name is Barack *Hussein* Obama."

The next evening, Joseph Farah, the editor of the conservative website WorldNetDaily, declared in a dinner speech, "I have a dream. And my dream is that if Barack Obama even seeks reelection as president in 2012, he won't be able to go to any city, any town, any hamlet in America without seeing signs that ask, 'Where's the birth certificate?'"

The birth of Jesus is better documented than that of Barack
Obama, Farah asserted, "even if there were no birth certifi-
cates two thousand years ago in Israel."

The delegates laughed the way they might at the crazy
uncle at the Thanksgiving table. Some people exchanged
glances; this was not what they wanted to talk about. Elsewhere at the convention, people had walked out of a session
after finding too much emphasis on prayer. Yet when Farah
concluded his speech asking, "Are you ready to engage in a
culture war after we take back Congress?" the room hollered
back, "*Yes!*"

Neither could Tea Partiers agree on who spoke for them.
Just outside the convention's ballrooms, a small group of men
staged their own press conference, objecting to Judson Phillips's attempt to stake a claim to Tea Party leadership by organizing this convention. "The Tea Party movement has no
leader," said Anthony Shreeve, a former associate of Phillips.
"It's a We the People movement."

Other groups objected to Phillips's group, Tea Party Nation,
because it was a for-profit corporation. Tea Party Patriots had
sent its members a note saying that it would not support the
convention because of the high ticket prices; it recommended
"thoroughly researching the convention before purchasing a
ticket."

Jenny Beth Martin, who did not attend the convention,
complained that even though she was back home in Atlanta,
she had spent all day answering questions about the Tea Party's
stance on social issues and Barack Obama's birth certificate. "I
thought we weren't going to be about social issues," she said.
And she objected to the personal nature of the attacks in
Nashville. "I understand there are people in the movement
who are frustrated with the things the president has done,"

she said. "The thing is, he can't sign any bills until they get through Congress. It's a battle about issues, not about personalities."

Tea Party organizers were suspicious of anyone who claimed to be a leader, and they spotted takeover attempts almost everywhere. When the Republican National Committee put up a website using Tea Party imagery, a group of Tea Partiers requested a meeting with Michael Steele, the party's chairman, to complain. Other Tea Party groups feared that this very meeting would be portrayed as cooperation between the Tea Party and the Republican Party; they issued a letter denouncing those who had requested the meeting as faux Tea Partiers.

The suspicion even tripped up Sarah Palin, who had seemed to be the Tea Party homecoming queen.

Her speech in Nashville was the high point of the convention; people lined up two hours before the ballroom doors opened to get a glimpse of her. She gave the crowd what they wanted, declaring, "America is ready for a revolution!" She hailed Scott Brown as representing "what this beautiful movement is all about. He was just a guy with a truck and a passion to serve our country." She called for a return to Tenth Amendment limits on government powers, complained about bailouts and the "generational theft" of rising deficits, and urged Tea Partiers to fight for conservative challengers against Republicans in primaries. By the end, the crowd was standing on chairs, chanting "Run, Sarah, run!"

"I've never met Ronald Reagan," Judson Phillips told the crowd, "But I've met Sarah Palin."

But the next day, Tea Party Patriots issued a press release declaring the convention to be a poor representation of the Tea Party, and complaining about "heavy efforts underway to align us to a political party."

"The Tea Party Movement started because of these tactics and we will not be used like this," it said. "We the People are smart and will not buy any tactics by politicians to use or co-opt us or the movement."

Palin's offense was her answer to a softball question that Phillips asked after her speech, about how she saw the future of the Tea Party movement. "The Republican Party would be really smart to start trying to absorb as much of the Tea Party movement as possible," she replied.

The Tea Partiers were feeling their power. They had worked too hard to earn this moment, and they were not about to concede the fight to any Republican, not even to Sarah Palin.

CHAPTER SIX

"We've kind of changed the rules"

"Okay: victory," Jennifer Stefano began. "You must win. Every single one of you. You must win, win, win, win, win. If you don't win on May 18, you may as well bang your head against a wall."

She stood before about thirty people jammed into tables in the front room of a restaurant that had not yet opened for the evening, its full-length curtains drawn against the bright spring Sunday afternoon outside. Some came dressed from family brunches, others in the drawstring shorts and sneakers that hinted at the lawns and Little Leagues they were missing. Six weeks until primary day, and the mission was clear.

"We're not here to talk about cap-and-trade; we're not here to talk about candidates or endorsements or illegal immigration. It's about winning," Stefano said. "We have to stay on track and stay on message."

They listened for two hours, taking notes on legal pads pulled from briefcases or leather portfolios, asking questions and sharing suggestions. Try handing out pencils with your name on it, one person said, or maps—"Everyone wants a map."

Finally, Stefano tried a little call-and-response to recap. "Our strategy right now is to . . . ," she said, waiting for the answer.

"Win," they replied.

"You sound like Democrats," she scolded. Louder: "What's our strategy?"

"To *WIN!*"

It had been nearly a year since Stefano and her husband and baby had happened upon the Tea Party in Washington Crossing Historic Park in Bucks County, Pennsylvania. Now six months pregnant with her second child, she wore white pants and a chic black top over her bump, her blonde hair swept back, a string of coral beads from Old Navy at her throat. She had become vice president of the Thomas Jefferson Club, the local Tea Party she had joined at her first rally. But that had not been enough to satisfy her ambition for change. She had recently started a group she called the Conservative Leadership Coalition, to identify and raise money for promising young candidates. And now she was trying to take over the entrenched ranks of the local Republican Party. The people in this room were her foot soldiers.

Like many others, Jennifer Stefano had been drawn to the Tea Party movement for its patriotism, for the sense of community, and because it was a place to find people who shared her concern about the country's growing debt and how it threatened the nation's security.

But her determination and her aims had sharpened in the past year. Tax Day was coming up, and she thought there might be a rally in Philadelphia, but she wasn't sure she was going. She was focused on other things, which she explained by recalling a lesson she had learned from Barney Frank, the

Democratic congressman from Massachusetts who was openly gay, proudly liberal, and an emblem of everything the right hated about the left. She had read about Frank addressing a gay rights group, taking its members to task for their protests and flamboyant parades. "He was saying, you're ridiculous, tripping down the streets. You've got to lobby, you've got to get elected," she recalled.

"Obviously Barney Frank and I could not be on more opposite sides on just about any subject," Stefano added. "But he's right. We have to use our resources and our energy and our intellect wisely. To me, that is getting people elected, getting political novices to get experience, and continuing to educate people on how to really change things. We're saber rattlers now, but after a while you will just be a noisemaker in a political landscape littered with them."

Stefano had started out more willing than many Tea Partiers to work with the Republican Party. But a year of activism had taught her that the local party officials did not want to work with the Tea Party. She now realized that before she could join the battle against the Democrats, she would have to get rid of another obstacle: the Republicans. Frustrated with the establishment, she had decided to become the establishment—or rather, to replace it. She filed papers to run for two local Republican committee positions—as a Bucks County representative to the state Republican Party, and as the committeewoman for her local precinct—and she recruited one hundred other conservatives to do the same.

The precinct positions are so low-level that in many parts of the country they are filled by the first people who show up, if they're filled at all. But here, in a district where Democrats and Republicans had fiercely battled for swing voters, the party infrastructure was well established, and most of the positions were contested. The Republican Party establishment was backing the incumbents, meaning that Stefano's recruits would have to outcampaign the machine. She was spending weekends training them on the basics, which is what had brought her to the restaurant on this Sunday afternoon.

Stefano had gotten two sympathetic Republicans—one a committee member, one a former member—to help. They told the people gathered that most voters stop checking off their ballots by the time they get down to the committee candidates, so you could win your precinct slot by as few as 60 or 125 votes. They gave the candidates a list of names and addresses for Republicans in their area, along with scripts for calling, writing, and going door-to-door. "Every call, every letter, mention the date of the election," Stefano reminded them. The committee members also told the candidates how to search the lists to identify supervoters—those who vote in almost every election, not just the big ones for president or governor. You must make contact with every one of those voters, they insisted, and follow up with a handwritten note. "You would be surprised how far that would take you to winning," one said.

Stefano gave the recruits no illusions about the office they were seeking. It was the lowest possible post in the party hierarchy. But she also pointed out that the committee people from the precincts elect the party executives in the county, who in turn decide which candidates to endorse and elect the state leadership, which ultimately elects the leadership of the Republican National Committee.

"The face of the new conservative leaders?" Stefano said to her crowd. "Congratulations. You're it."

Lots of Tea Partiers were just as angry at Republicans as they were at Democrats. For twelve years following the Republican Revolution of 1994, the party had held nearly unbroken control of Congress, but it hadn't worked out to be much of a revolution. Despite all the promises of term limits and cutting waste and paying-as-you-go that were contained in the Contract with America, spending still skyrocketed, government still grew.

Conservatives complained about officeholders and candidates who were "Republicans in Name Only," or RINOs, by which they meant moderates who supported abortion rights and gay marriage. To Tea Partiers, the RINOs were the ones who were not serious about cutting spending, who had supported the Medicare expansion under President Bush and the Republican-controlled Congress, or, more recently, who had supported the stimulus or made bipartisan overtures toward health care reform or cap-and-trade—which Tea Partiers called "cap-and-tax," believing that energy companies would simply pass on the cost of buying carbon credits to their customers.

But these were not the centrist voters who went for Ross Perot in the 1990s, casting a pox on both parties' houses; the Republican Party was still the closest resting place for them. Like Jennifer Stefano, many Tea Partiers held conservative views on issues like abortion, and they certainly did not share the Democrats' desire to expand social programs like health care. Most of them did not seek to form a third party that would nominate candidates to run in general elections. They remembered the ultimate failure of Perot's movement, which allowed the Democratic candidate for president, Bill Clinton, to win in 1992 and 1996 with less than half the popular vote. Some went so far as to dismiss suggestions of a third party as an attempt by the left to sabotage the strength of the Tea Party.

What they wanted instead was to remake the Republican Party in the Tea Party's image: in favor of less-invasive government, lower taxes, and fealty to the view of the nation the founders enshrined in the Constitution. In the months ahead, the Tea Party's energy would be brought to bear against the Democrats in the 2010 midterm elections. But in the long term, any "Second American Revolution" was going to be within the ranks of the Republican Party itself. "I think we can do greater things working in a system that's established than we ever can being a bunch of anarchists," Stefano said.

In some places, Tea Partiers were fighting the Republican establishment by backing conservative candidates in Republican primaries. In Florida, the realization that he did not have the conservative support needed to win the Republican primary drove Charlie Crist out of the primary, to run for the Senate as an independent. In Utah, Tea Partiers massed at the state Republican convention to deny renomination for a fourth term to Senator Robert Bennett, after he supported the bank bailout and proposed health care legislation that would have required people to purchase health insurance.

Other Tea Party groups were holding candidate forums to try to weed out candidates who did not share their values. The Independence Caucus, a Utah-based group that helped drive out Senator Bennett, produced a questionnaire that many Tea Party groups across the country used to vet candidates before endorsing them. The survey asked eighty questions, including a candidate's position on *Wickard v. Filburn*, the Tenth Amendment, and James Madison's ideas governing budgets, as expressed in *The Federalist Papers*. (The questionnaire asked no questions on "faith" or "family," the hot-button words that had dominated the conservative discussion for four decades.)

But under the radar, the Tea Partiers had figured out that

if they wanted to stop the Republican Party from backing candidates like Dede Scozzafava or Charlie Crist, the long-term solution was to install true conservatives in party offices. So across the country they were doing the same thing Jennifer Stefano was doing in Bucks County, recruiting Tea Party people to fill the lowest-level posts in the hope that they could take over the party from the ground up.

With the rallying cry, "No more NY-23!" word of the precinct strategy spread online and at Tea Party events where there were seminars on how to take over the party, starting with the local committee. Its proponents called the precinct job the most important office in the country—the building block of the entire party. Barack Obama, they reminded their fellow Tea Partiers, had won the Democratic presidential nomination in 2008 by recruiting enthusiastic precinct captains to get out the vote in primaries and caucuses. This strategy was also similar to the tactics used by Christian conservatives in the early 1990s, winning seats on school boards and other local bodies, and by the supporters of Howard Dean, who had taken over some state Democratic parties after his unsuccessful but galvanizing campaign for the presidential nomination in 2004.

"It can only be done one county at a time, one state at a time," said Philip Glass, a former commercial mortgage banker in Cincinnati who started the National Precinct Alliance with Tea Party members he met online and at Tea Party seminars. "But even if you've got a slight majority—you just need maybe twenty-six states—then you can have your say in how the party goes."

The activists' mantra reflected an easy confidence in the strategy: take the precinct, take the state, take the party. The alliance recruited a coordinator in every state to help identify

Tea Party activists to fill the positions. "We want to fill every seat in the party with essentially our people," Glass said. "This cycle I doubt that's going to happen, but by the next cycle there is a really good possibility."

In precincts where positions had gone unfilled, the requirements for joining the Republican committee were often minimal. Very often, all that candidates had to do was to collect as few as ten signatures, or just show up for two meetings. And they were making their presence felt very quickly. In Maricopa County, Arizona, Tea Party candidates filled 545 empty positions in the local committee, swelling its numbers to 3,030. The new recruits then flooded the annual meeting and elected a conservative slate of officers. And then in a straw poll for the U.S. Senate race, the kind of event that carries no weight but can build a narrative for or against a candidacy, the Maricopa County Republicans overwhelmingly chose the conservative challenger, J. D. Hayworth, a talk radio host and former congressman, over John McCain, the incumbent and the party's 2008 presidential nominee.

In Las Vegas, a takeover started when about thirty activists who had become friendly from Tea Party protests got together to discuss how to turn their activism into political power. They were eager to defeat Harry Reid, the Democrats' leader in the Senate, but they did not trust the Republican Party to back the right candidate. One activist mentioned that there were about five hundred empty spots on the local Republican committee. "We didn't even know how the darn party worked," said Tony Warren, another activist, who would later help Philip Glass start the National Precinct Alliance. Just by attending meetings, they expanded the ranks of the Clark County Republican Committee by three hundred members. Then they elected an executive committee dominated by conservatives, and because Clark County holds the bulk of Nevada's population, they were able to elect a conservative slate to the state party leadership, too.

But in places like Bucks County, Pennsylvania, where Jennifer Stefano was trying to engineer a takeover, the committee positions tended to be occupied, so it was more of a fight. Some establishment Republicans did not want to relinquish control. Others worried about letting conservatives pull the party to the right when the conventional wisdom about winning elections is that candidates have to appeal to the middle.

Tea Partiers argued instead that the Republicans had to stand for something.

"We're not just against something, the men and women I speak to, it's not just 'Obama, yuck,'" Stefano said. "We're not gun-toting religious nut-job racists. We're well informed, well educated. We just want to set the course. We want to go back to the fundamentals of what the Republicans stand for: small government, strong national defense, and strong foreign policy."

Jennifer Stefano had tried to get involved with Republican politics during the 2008 presidential campaign. She could not summon much enthusiasm for John McCain, but she bristled at Barack Obama's comments about white working-class voters that were captured on tape at a private fundraiser in San Francisco just before her state's primary. Talking about places in Pennsylvania that had been bleeding jobs and watching promises of government help evaporate, he said, "It's not surprising, then, they get bitter, they cling to guns or religion or antipathy to people who aren't like them or anti-immigrant sentiment or anti-trade sentiment as a way to explain their frustrations."

Stefano felt like he could have been talking about her. And she didn't like it.

"I get the sense from Barack Obama that he doesn't like the people he's seeking to represent," she said. "I really believe that a lot of these people think that someone like me—a college-educated woman, I've worked all my life—that I'm an oppressor, a racist."

She wanted to find a way to turn her frustration into action, so she decided to try to learn from the experts: MoveOn. "I wanted to see what they were doing, to see if I could find the equivalent," she recalled. "I was like, where is the MoveOn on the right?"

She phoned and emailed Republican headquarters. "Anyone who was a Republican I tried to reach out to," she said. "The silence was deafening." Finally, someone asked her to come to the local party headquarters to make phone calls. "There was another woman there. I said, 'This is ridiculous.' MoveOn was at the polls, they're working the streets. We were making phone calls in some room and this was going to get us to victory? There was nothing on the ground. Nothing."

Obama's election only hardened her resolve. "He and Bush grew the national debt to unacceptable, unacceptable levels and in doing so have literally made us beholden to the people who are our enemies, to people who don't respect democracy," she said. "Look at the oil exporters who own us—Saudi Arabia, Venezuela. Look at China, their human rights record.

"Barack Obama's fatal mistake was that he came between me and my child's future. And the Republicans failed to put up a defense."

Stumbling on the Tea Party that afternoon in Washington Crossing Park, she thought, "This is not the future I imagined for myself. But it is now."

Stefano was emblematic of a striking trend: A significant portion of the Tea Party organizers were women, in a movement that nearly every poll suggested was supported mostly by men. A lot of these women felt called to action and spoke, as Stefano did, as mothers, concerned for their children's future. Jenny Beth Martin had once spent much of her time blogging about her family from her home in Atlanta; now she was on television as the face of Tea Party Patriots. A majority of the activists on her Monday night conference calls were women, too. Glenn Beck's 9/12 project had produced a spinoff, a "Sisterhood of Mommy Patriots" called As a Mom. The name came from the comment of one of Beck's guests on his Fox News show, the veteran Republican pollster and image-maker Frank Luntz, who advised, "If you begin everything with, 'As a mom . . . ,' you win." And in Bucks County, the organizer of the first rally at Washington Crossing, Anastasia Przybylski, described herself as "just a stay-at-home mom."

Eight months after that rally, in December 2009, the Bucks County Tea Party groups had seemed to be making inroads with the local Republican establishment. Pat Poprik, the cochairwoman of the local committee, called to invite them to a meeting. The Tea Party groups were eager to discuss the upcoming congressional race against Patrick Murphy, a thirty-six-year-old Iraq War veteran who had won the seat in the Democratic sweep of 2006 and retained it in the Obama election of 2008.

Poprik told them that the committee members—about five hundred people—would meet with the Republican candidates seeking to take on Murphy in early March. Those committee members would vote on their preferences and then send their recommendations to the executive committee— about ninety people—who would vote on an endorsement. The endorsed candidate's name would be checked off on the official Republican ballots that the committee mailed and handed out to voters to advise them as they went to the polls.

Przybylski suggested that the committee not make an endorsement at all. Several candidates, many of them brought to politics by the Tea Party, had already lined up to run, she said. Why not see if any of them would take off? An open primary could build excitement—the Republicans might criticize each other, but every time one of them spoke they would be highlighting the sins of Patrick Murphy. With all the grassroots excitement, it did not seem right that fewer than a hundred people would choose the party's nominee. And given the anti-establishment mood, it might discourage people from voting if they thought the establishment had minted the candidate. "We don't want to see what happened in New York happen here," Przybylski said.

Poprik countered that a competitive primary could be divisive. "We feel that it is our job to recommend someone," she said. "There are so many voters who don't meet the people who are running. They trust their party for a recommendation." She added that there was nothing stopping someone from mounting a primary challenge to the candidate receiving the executive committee's endorsement.

But Mike Fitzpatrick, a former congressman who had narrowly lost to Murphy in 2006, was likely to run again. It was an open secret that the party was planning to back him; in 2008, the Republicans had figured they didn't have a chance against the Democrats, but the shift in energy over the last several months had given them hope that a strong candidate could take back the seat. The Tea Party groups thought that the Republican committee's imprimatur, along with Fitzpatrick's name recognition, would make it folly for anyone else to run for the seat.

Przybylski left the meeting frustrated. She had changed her voter registration a few years earlier from Democrat to Republican so she could vote in a primary. "What's the point of even being registered Republican and not Independent?" she said. "If there's always an endorsement, what's the point, really? The parties have all done this the same way, and people didn't notice. We all thought we were voting and there was just one person to vote for."

More important, Przybylski was underwhelmed by Fitz-patrick. The party leaders had chosen him to run for the seat in 2004 largely because of his strong opposition to abortion. But she didn't think that the abortion issue was a winner for the Tea Party. "I have friends where that's a big turnoff," she said. "They're registered Democrats because of abortion, but they're totally freaking out about the debt."

The Republican committee, she said, was not emphasizing fiscal conservatism when it chose to endorse a candidate. "Win-nability is emphasized," she said. "There's something to that. At the same time, if someone is completely against what the policies of the party are, in good conscience, you can't sup-port someone like that."

The Tea Party groups decided that they would just have to strip the endorsement of some of its punch. They made plans to hold a candidate forum where the audience would be able to cast ballots for their preferred candidates. They would hold a series of candidate debates to force a discussion between the endorsed and non-endorsed candidates.

"If they're not going to have a primary, we're going to create one," Przybylski said. "We've kind of changed the rules."

On a bitter January night, a standing-room-only crowd filled the auditorium of Council Rock South High School for the candidate forum. It was a wood-paneled space with a professional sound system, one that would not have been out of place on a college campus, and reflected the local taxpayers' investment in their schools.

Nine candidates showed up, one in a rented truck displaying billboards for his campaign. Mike Fitzpatrick did not.

Anastasia Przybylski and the other organizers had decided to call the candidates onto the stage individually to be questioned by a local television anchor, hoping this would require them to explain their views more fully, rather than just agreeing with what everyone else on stage had said.

The questions hinted at the mix of libertarian and conservative concerns in Tea Party ideology: Will you pledge to vote against tax increases, even hidden taxes, such as those contained in the health care reform bill? Will you lead the fight to drill for oil in American fields? Should corporate executives who encourage illegal aliens to stay because it's good for business be hauled off to jail? Do you believe man-made pollution is a significant contributor to global warming? ("I don't necessarily think there's been global warming," one candidate objected.)

The candidates were asked whether they agreed with the Obama administration's directive that federal officials should not prosecute people who use medicinal marijuana in states that allow it. Most said yes. When asked "Should *Roe v. Wade* be weakened?" all but one candidate answered, "No."

Each was asked to define the Tenth Amendment, and to give examples of where it "might have been violated."

"It's my favorite amendment in the Constitution!" exclaimed one candidate, Ira Hoffman. "I can't believe it!"

He cited the New Deal as one example of a violation and the current push for health care legislation as another. Then, like the other candidates, he was asked if he would back efforts to nullify any health care legislation that was passed. "When I see thirteen attorney generals on television saying they're suing, I turn up the volume," he said. "I love it." He said he would start fresh in reforming health care, emphasizing tort reform, offering health savings accounts, and making it tax-deductible for individuals to buy health insurance.

Finally, the moderator asked everyone if 2010 would be "the year of the Tea Party." Everyone agreed, at least in part.

"It depends," offered Tom Lingenfelter, a historian with a slightly absent-minded-professor look who had been handing out pocket Constitutions before the forum. "The party bosses have picked the candidates across the state. They always endorse a candidate. Endorsing a candidate is tantamount to anointing him. The candidate has already been chosen, and he's not here tonight."

Jennifer Stefano, in the audience, nodded her head vigorously. "Finally someone said it," she said under her breath. "Fitzpatrick is disrespecting the movement—that could hurt him. This movement does not have enough power right now on its own to get a candidate to victory. But this movement certainly has the power to make candidates lose, even if they're backed."

Two weeks later, with anger among Tea Partiers mounting, Mike Fitzpatrick called for an open primary, with the party withholding any endorsement. "I am running to be the people's candidate and I believe an open process will improve participation and lead to a higher level of debate," he told the local newspaper.

Pat Poprik told the paper that the fuss over the endorsement

was "baffling" to her. But she said she would relay Fitzpatrick's recommendation to her committee members. "It may
be something the party would consider," she said. "I don't
know."

Stefano, who was running simultaneously for the local
committee and to be one of Bucks County's representatives
to the state party, was losing patience in her battle with the
Republican establishment. Over the months, you could hear
her irritation with the party growing.

"I am not the enemy, I am not looking to overthrow them
or anything like that," she said in January. "I guess I just have
a level of frustration. People like me in the Tea Party, why
wouldn't you make us your allies?"

A few months later, as she prepared to train her recruits,
she criticized the party for "this sense of having to wait your
turn."

"They're not particularly thrilled with people like me,"
she said. "I don't know who likes us less, the Democrats or the
establishment Republicans. I don't care."

She had big goals about making the party more assertive.
"The lower end of Bucks County is heavily Democratic," she
said. "We have to go out and start bringing the message to the
people, recruiting people to run for vacant seats there. Democratic areas, working- and middle-class places, the conservative message has to be taken there."

But first, her people had to win.

⌒

The restaurant where the candidates for committee positions
had gathered was just off the historic center of Newtown,
Pennsylvania. At one end of nearby Washington Avenue was a

precise parade of colonial homes flying American flags, at the other were new houses for sale at a Toll Brothers development.

Stefano had recruited the owner of the restaurant to run for the Republican committee, and the owner had agreed to let her use the space for training. "My new favorite people, you're on time," Stefano said as her recruits arrived.

Kathy Suntato, a bookkeeper whose husband was retired, said that taxes were her main issue in running. She had campaigned for a school board candidate who had promised to limit tax increases, and it felt good. "At some point you decide that if you don't do something, it's not going to end spending," she said.

She had been a Democrat for thirty years, then an independent, and she had registered as a Republican just before the cutoff date to run for the committee position, having heard about it at a Thomas Jefferson Club event. "I'm all about government having no debt," she said. "It doesn't matter whether they call themselves a Tea Party. What is a Tea Party, really? Anyone that's mad."

"I'd say concerned," interrupted Bernadette Repisky, a forty-six-year-old stay-at-home mother. "This has never happened before, that people felt so concerned for the well-being of this country. It's like Santelli said, 'I'm fed up, I'm surprised people aren't going to start throwing tea in the harbor or something.'"

As waiters set votive candles on white tablecloths in an adjacent room, a Sade song playing in the background, Stefano began. She encouraged people to keep it simple: "It's not about getting endorsements. It's not about writing position papers. Think of where you were six months ago. If someone had said they want to audit the Fed or block cap-and-trade, you wouldn't have known what they were talking about and you wouldn't have voted for them. This is about meeting your neighbors. Meet and know your neighbors, and talk to them."

"Have I gotten doors slammed in my face? Yes, two," she said. "It's hard. But we not only have better ideas, we have better manners. It's really really important that we remember that. We want to have grace, dignity, class. Because God knows no one else running this country does."

Stefano then introduced Steve Gotkis, a retiring committeeperson who had agreed to help pass on tips about campaigning.

"How many of you have ever had a Republican committee person knock on your door?" he said. Two hands went up. "That's the problem with the current Bucks County Republican Party," Gotkis said. "I call them the heritage types. They're Republican committee people because their mother and father were Republican committee people."

Gotkis and Stefano walked the candidates through the scripts they had written for emails, phone calls, door knocking, and personalized letters. "My job will be to represent your voice and views to the local Republican Party," the door-knocking script read. The email one dictated: "As your voice in the Republican Party, I will work to: promote small government ideals; cut spending to keep taxes low; support our small businesses and local entrepreneurs."

"You're going to win if you do this," Stefano said. "Don't deviate. That's it."

Call everyone you know, they advised. "As soon as you leave this meeting," Gotkis urged. The best time for door knocking is between six and eight o'clock, and on weekends. Every candidate can have two poll watchers, but you have to find a friendly committee person to appoint them for you.

Keli Carender (*right*) led the first Tea Party protest in February 2009, in Seattle. The Tea Party movement coalesced around activists like her, with individual resourcefulness helped along by conservative media personalities like Kirby Wilbur (*left*), a radio host shown with Carender at a later rally in Olympia, Washington. (Kevin P. Casey/*The New York Times*)

On February 19, 2009, from the floor of the Chicago Mercantile Exchange, the financial-news commentator Rick Santelli launched into a "rant" against mortgage bailouts, broadcast across the country on the cable network CNBC. "We're thinking of having a Chicago Tea Party here," he said, providing a rallying cry and a name for the first big wave of protests a week later. (Courtesy of CNBC)

Glenn Beck, the Fox News anchor famous for promoting conservative politics and ridiculing liberal ideas, hosted a special episode of his show in March 2009, encouraging his viewers to form "9/12 groups," his brand of Tea Party, to get back to the unity of purpose the country felt on the day after the September 11 attacks. (Nicholas Roberts/ *The New York Times*)

Former House Majority Leader Dick Armey, shown here brandishing his trademark Stetson hat, is the chairman of FreedomWorks, a conservative advocacy group that had been trying to rally a grassroots antitax movement for years. As the Tea Party movement spread in the late winter and early spring of 2009, FreedomWorks quickly moved to mobilize anger and fear about bank and automobile industry bailouts, the economic stimulus, and the health care overhaul. (Brendan Smialowski/*The New York Times*)

Signs and costumes in the crowd at the 9/12 march on the Capitol in September 2009 show the protesters' influences, from the Founding Fathers to Fox News. (Amanda Lucidon/*The New York Times*)

Brendan Steinhauser, a young staffer at FreedomWorks, proudly called himself a "community organizer," taking inspiration from left-wing icons like Saul Alinsky and Bayard Rustin. (Photo courtesy of Brendan Steinhauser)

FreedomWorks organizers called the march "the largest conservative protest in American history." (Amanda Lucidon/*The New York Times*)

On January 19, 2010, a little-known Republican state senator named Scott Brown won the special election to fill the U.S. Senate seat in Massachusetts that had been held by Ted Kennedy. Brown's stunning upset showed the strength of the Tea Party forces and convinced the movement's leaders that they could take any seat in the country, with enough organization and determination. (Bryce Vickmark/*The New York Times*)

At the victory party, Scott Brown's supporters waved the "flag of the Second American Revolution," designed by Jeff McQueen, a Tea Partier from Michigan, featuring thirteen stars in a circle with the roman numeral II in the center. The flag had become a prominent emblem at Tea Party rallies since the summer of 2009. (Bryce Vickmark/*The New York Times*)

Two weeks after Brown's victory, on February 6, 2010, Sarah Palin paid tribute to the Tea Party movement before an adoring crowd at the inaugural National Tea Party Convention in Nashville, proclaiming, "America is ready for another revolution!" Still, most Tea Party supporters did not consider Palin qualified to be president. (Stephen Crowley/*The New York Times*)

Local Tea Party leaders like Anastasia Przybylski, shown at a candidate forum she organized outside Philadelphia in January 2010, began trying to take over the Republican Party from the ground up. (Jessica Kourkounis/*The New York Times*)

The movement became a social community as well as a political cause, and activists like Diana Reimer of Lansdale, Pennsylvania, shown here while lobbying on Capitol Hill with another activist leader, Ben Tessler, embraced it with near-religious fervor. (Stephen Crowley/*The New York Times*)

Tea Partiers embraced an originalist view of the Constitution as the backbone of their opposition to a growing government role in the economy and health care. Here, protesters consult a guide to the founding document. (Jim Wilson/*The New York Times*)

Polls—and signs like this one at a Tea Party rally—showed a more emotional opposition to President Barack Obama among Tea Party supporters. (Jim Wilson/ *The New York Times*)

Hundreds of cars and RVs flooded a newly cleared swath of desert outside Searchlight, Nevada, for a Tea Party rally in March 2010 against Senator Harry Reid, the Democratic majority leader, who was in a tough race for reelection to the U.S. Senate. (Jim Wilson/*The New York Times*)

The protesters were welcomed to town by a billboard mocking Senator Reid. (Jim Wilson/*The New York Times*)

Opposition to the health care legislation remained a driving force for the Tea Party movement as it turned its attention to the 2010 midterm elections, as seen in these signs carried at a Tax Day rally in Sacramento, California. (Jim Wilson/*The New York Times*)

Rand Paul, running in the Republican primary for the U.S. Senate in Kentucky, was a test case for Tea Party supporters; he shared their ideology and had the name recognition to raise money, but many establishment Republicans feared he could not win the general election and supported his opponent, Trey Grayson. (Kevin Riddell/*The New York Times*)

Take absentee ballots with you when you go door to door. And collect email addresses—the goal was for the group to grow its list to 15,000 people by primary day.

"We'll do a lit drop before the primary," Gotkis said.

"A what drop?"

"A literature drop," he explained, a sample ballot with the names of the challengers checked off to counter the "official" sample ballot the Republican Party would hand out with its candidates for the committee positions checked off.

The candidates were also told that they should not hand out literature for congressional candidates or for other campaigns. "The most important election is this one," Stefano said. "If we can win this committee, we can stop this corrupt party insider dealing where they make endorsements and we don't get a voice."

"Questions?" Gotkis asked.

"Questions about winning," Stefano corrected him.

What do the committee people actually do? someone asked.

They vote for the local leaders, who vote for the state leaders, who vote for the national leaders. But most important, Stefano and Gotkis said, it was about influence. You were the pulse of the Republicans in your district; you let the committee know what voters wanted and let voters know what the committee was doing.

"The average voter has an appalling degree of knowledge about elections," said Gotkis. "They ask you who to vote for, and you can tell them."

⌐

Stefano and a handful of other candidates running for the state positions stayed late to plot strategy.

Andy Raffle, the former committee person Stefano had asked to help with training, had brought his laptop to show off the sample ballot he had designed for the literature drop, with the names of the conservative challengers to the committee checked off. "We the People," read the logo at the top. Underneath was a platform: Promote small government ideals. Cut spending to keep taxes low. No primary endorsements, so voters decide.

Stefano suggested getting rid of "We the People" in favor of making the names bigger. "I don't want Tea Party on it," she said. "No rhetoric."

She also suggested deleting the line about primary endorsements and replacing it with something about supporting small businesses. "Six months ago I would not have known what that is," she said. "I don't think it means anything to people."

The most important thing is campaigning at the polls, she said. "Be the last person someone speaks with before they vote. Don't hand them something, hand them your hand: 'Is the Republican Party working for you?'"

She mentioned that she had started the Conservative Leadership Coalition to develop a new generation of conservative leaders, at all levels. "We have got to start helping Republican leaders to help them get elected," she said. "We've got to find out who the hell they are, people with our values. It kills me, Barack Obama gets elected and who do we have for fresh blood? Who are you recruiting, who are you training?"

"In 1994 we had new people," Gotkis said, reminding her of all the young ideological Republicans who had come in during the last Republican Revolution. "They decided to become like Democrats."

Raffle said they had to start by finding people who were on the right side of local issues. "We're all concerned with cap-

and-trade, but responsible contract ordinances are important, too," he said. "Local, local, local. Start recruiting candidates for the school board, then they can move up."

"We have to go and find these people," Stefano agreed. "The only way to get rid of Democrats is to get rid of the Republicans."

CHAPTER SEVEN

"It's a mission"

In early 2009, when Diana Reimer was a saleswoman in the moderate sportswear department of the Macy's near her suburban Philadelphia home, worried mostly about whether she and her husband could sell their three-bedroom split-level, she figured she had been to the nation's capital once, perhaps twice, in her sixty-six years. Maybe to show some houseguests the sights, but she couldn't remember exactly.

Now, a year later, she was commuting to Washington often, having quit her job to become a full-time Tea Party volunteer, a major in the FreedomWorks army and a national coordinator for Tea Party Patriots. Normally she took a five A.M. commuter train and switched in Philadelphia to arrive at Union Station before nine o'clock. But Tuesday, March 16, was a big day—Scott Brown's win had not stopped the health care bill after all, and Tea Party Patriots had put out an email that people should come to Washington to lobby against it. So Reimer had taken the train the previous afternoon to set up at the Capitol Hill Hyatt, a place where politicians hold their victory parties on election night.

By 8:30 that morning, she had already finished a meeting with the other national coordinators, and her birdlike frame could be seen rushing across the Capitol grounds to find the place where she was to direct the citizen lobbyists coming in for the day. She stopped on the east lawn, where Jenny Beth Martin was using a bullhorn to rally about fifty people who'd gathered. Then, turning a corner, she bumped into Steve King, a Republican congressman from Iowa and a frequent speaker at Tea Party rallies. "Diana!" he exclaimed, enveloping her in a bear hug. "I should have known you'd be here!"

Crossing the street, Reimer found the meeting place and hugged Brendan Steinhauser of FreedomWorks, who was handing out the packets with talking points that the organization had drawn up. Then she hugged her friend Kevin Kelly, whom she had met organizing Tea Parties in Philadelphia, and her new friend Ben Tessler. She was planning to stay over again that night to help Tessler run the first meeting of a new Tea Party group for the Washington area.

"You're a ball of fire," Tessler told her. "All we have to do is call a joint session of Congress, put you in there and lock the door. There's no way they could pass it."

"Oh gosh," Reimer said, laughing. "I don't know."

A small group that had responded to the Tea Party alert had gathered to go into the Capitol. Among them was a man wearing a clown costume, shouting and carrying a sign reading PELOSI SPITS IN AMERICA'S FACE. Reimer looked over with distaste. "We don't do stuff like that," she said. "That's what gives us a bad name. He could be a plant. Absolutely. They'll do anything to make us look bad because they think we're radicals. They'll do absolutely anything."

It was a cold, not-quite-spring day, and she stood shivering in a pink turtleneck as she checked her pink BlackBerry for updates on the buses that were supposed to arrive from Philadelphia and handed out packets to the people beginning to gather outside the House office buildings.

"The room numbers are in there, with some talking points," she instructed, unfailingly cheerful, unfailingly polite. "We're thanking the ones voting no, and encouraging the ones voting yes to change their minds."

"Diana? Diana Reimer?" one woman said, taking the materials. "Wow. It's nice to meet you in person."

A man in a cap reading ONCE A MARINE, ALWAYS A MARINE hailed her: "Our slave driver!" She laughed, recognizing him as a man from North Carolina who had knocked on doors with her in the snows of suburban Boston for the Scott Brown campaign two months earlier.

"Sometimes you don't know how many people you know until you come down here," Reimer said. "We have friends now across the country. It's amazing. It's amazing."

She and her husband, Don, had hoped to sell their house so they could pay down some debts. It hadn't helped that he was forced into retirement, and now that she had quit her job, they were relying on savings, dipping into it to pay for things like flags, hats, a sound system, and pocket versions of the Constitution to give away at their first Tea Party events.

"This is what we have to do," she said. "Even if I wanted to stop, I can't, I'm just driven. I'm on a mission, and time is not on my side, so I have a lot of work to do."

The Reimers had recently held a small fundraiser to make up some of the money they had spent. But Diana did not seem terribly concerned. Though she was not an especially religious person, she talked about her Tea Party work as a higher calling. "I think about it, but I feel God is in control and I feel this is what God wants me to do. He's going to take care of us."

She was working longer hours than ever, but she was happier than ever, too. "I love it, I love it," she said. "I don't know everything but I know more about politics than I ever did in my entire life."

It was something, she said, that the Tea Party's opponents did not understand. "They have to look at the real, real people," she said. "I mean, this is truly grassroots. There's a lot of us here working and doing and just, you know, just doing this and getting it done. I don't think they understand that somebody would put all this effort, all their energy into something like this and not get paid for it. They don't believe the passion behind the American people.

"I myself feel it's a God-driven passion, that's what I feel. I didn't wake up one morning and say I think I'm going to spend twelve hours on the computer. No, it's a mission. You're on a mission. To save this country, and help the American people."

Standing outside the Capitol in the cold, her eyes welled up.

"I get some phone calls and emails that really bring tears to my eyes," she said. "They just thank you for helping them to have a voice, to get out there. They've never done this before, it's something that—they just thank you so much. They were sitting there and now they're out there doing something and it makes them feel good. They're not doing anything wrong, they're standing up for their God-given right.

"I don't feel," she said, her voice breaking, "that I'm doing anything special. I feel I'm just doing what I have to do. You know? And that's—and everybody, well, you see the people. I'm respected. I don't know why, I don't know what is so special, but I'm willing to do it.

"I'm happy," she said, "I'm really happy. One way or the other it will work out. I couldn't imagine not doing this. This is now—this is my life."

To its activists, the Tea Party movement quickly became something more than protest. It was more like a religion. It had given them a community, and it had given them a cause, which they embraced like a crusade.

The language and the symbols of the movement helped encourage that sense of mission, the feeling that they were the true patriots. But for many people, there was enough appeal in simply having that community, a place to get out their frustrations. Outsiders who underestimated the movement failed to appreciate how much it had come to mean to those involved.

When the Sam Adams Alliance, a Chicago group supportive of the Tea Parties, conducted interviews with fifty leaders of Tea Party groups to determine their motivation, the respondents cited the most rewarding aspects of the Tea Party work as the "friendship" and the "fellowship." One woman said she got "addicted to the emotional high"; another said participating made her feel "less lonely" and that her voice was heard. A man explained that it was "one aspect of my life I can control."

"My life is worthwhile," one woman said, adding, "I gave up my business for this." Tea Party leaders handed out elaborate business cards with well-designed logos, pictures of eagles, quotations from Thomas Jefferson. The Sam Adams interviewers picked up a similar professionalism elsewhere.

Some leaders spoke of the need for the Tea Party to "brand better."

For all the ways the Tea Party could be Me the People—prizing individualism and wanting above all to protect private property—its activists believed in this fellowship, the idea of belonging to something greater. It was the analogy that Matt Kibbe at FreedomWorks had drawn to the Grateful Dead. He had never been ripped off at a Dead show, he noted; people looked out for one another and trusted virtual strangers on the basis of a shared bond—though there were undoubtedly some substances encouraging the love at a Dead show, substances that were not in evidence at Tea Party rallies. This shared bond created some unlikely relationships. Brendan Steinhauser counted Diana Reimer, four decades his senior, as a close friend. "No matter what happens we will always be close," he said. "That's the way it is with a lot of these guys. It's kind of like a family."

He encouraged the Tea Partiers to see one another as comrades in arms. "Don't forget the social aspects, these ties that bind us all," Steinhauser told participants at a Freedom-Works seminar. "There's something very powerful about that."

These were troops with a keen nose for the enemy. They believed that if anyone was guilty of Astroturf organizing, it was their opponents on the left, with the labor unions busing in protesters to rally for health care legislation, and they insisted that the most outrageous Tea Party signs were actually sent in by the left to make the Tea Party look bad. (There was little to prove this. The staff at FreedomWorks liked to point out, correctly, that the posters showing President Obama with a Hitler moustache were printed by the supporters of Lyndon LaRouche, the octogenarian political provocateur who had recently likened Obama's health care plan to the gas chambers of the Third Reich. "LaRouche fruitcakes," Dick Armey called them. "And we all know who the LaRouchies are," he added. "They're Democrats!")

The Tea Partiers' finely honed impression of Us versus Them made them see setbacks as anything but. A loss, whether in New York's Twenty-third Congressional District or on the health care bill, only reinforced their determination.

They believed unquestioningly that they were the nation's true silent majority: in the *New York Times*/CBS News poll, 84 percent of Tea Party supporters said that the movement reflected the views of most Americans, while only 25 percent of the general public said the same. Most of them said they were more likely to trust information from fellow supporters than they were what they heard on television or read in newspapers.

In that echo chamber, the Tea Partiers quickly went from feeling ignored to feeling persecuted. In the weeks before the House of Representatives voted on the final health care bill, Tea Party websites began to circulate a report from the Drudge Report and BigGovernment.com that said former President Bill Clinton and his longtime political consultant James Carville had a plan to identify top Tea Party leaders and "turn" one of them to create a mole in the movement, and then use that person to smear the rest. The stories did not identify any source ("BigGovernment has learned . . .") and Clinton himself was in the hospital having heart surgery, but the Tea Partiers wore the very thought of the legendary Democrats' scorn like a badge of honor. The left just didn't get it, they laughed—this movement wasn't about leaders, it was about *the people*. Tea Party Patriots encouraged its members to submit videos of themselves saying "I am the Tea Party leader!" to mock the cluelessness of the opposition.

The belief in a mission that Diana Reimer and others described is what made the health care debate so pitched. The Tea Partiers spoke of it as a battle not just of principle—plenty of people on the other side would have agreed it was that—but between righteousness and evil, between freedom and slavery. Those who tried to engage the Tea Partiers in debate about the details of the legislation—Should young people be able to stay on their parents' health insurance? Should insurance companies be required to cover people with preexisting conditions? Should there be health care exchanges instead of a public option?—seemed to be missing the point. To the Tea Partiers, it was an all-or-nothing struggle.

"What scares me about health care is that it's not about health care," Reimer said. "It's about control, and this is America the free."

Tom Grimes, the "bus czar" from South Bend, Indiana, wrote an email to a Tea Party friend in November 2009 after returning from an anti–health care demonstration in Washington, describing himself almost like Shakespeare's Henry V, spreading comfort among his weary soldiers.

"I felt like a stern but loving general preparing the troops for battle on the ride through the rolling hills of Pennsylvania," he wrote. "Early evening fell on the capital and my limping band of rebels returned from their mission. . . . They were uplifted emotionally and proud of their sacrifices, with both physical and mental pain boarded the bus only wanting to eat and sleep on the grueling ride back." He wrote of rallying others to lift a woman in a wheelchair over a three-and-a-half-foot wall so she could ascend the lawn in front of the Capitol. "I waved my platoon over with Pat in the wheelchair and said, 'We have no choice, this is it.'"

Grimes would later recall how he had been in a wheel-chair himself, suffering from sciatica, on the trip to Washington for the first 9/12 rally in September 2009. He was not sure he could march, but his friends insisted that they would push the chair through the streets of Washington. He wept, he said, at the charity of others. "I called my wife from my wheelchair and cried like when my dad had passed away," he said. "I've cried, but this—it was hard to stop bawling. I said to her, this is probably the most significant thing I've done in my life."

For some Tea Partiers, particularly the younger ones who came to the movement first, the passion for it began with unswerving ideology.

A year to the day after Keli Carender held the first Tea Party, she drove to the Washington state capitol in Olympia. She had become something of a local celebrity; at an antitax rally on the capitol steps, she was hailed by one of the speakers as the one who started it all. A television crew sought her out afterward. Kirby Wilbur, the conservative radio host who had helped promote Carender's first event, embraced her warmly, calling out, "The future of the conservative movement!"

In a bio she had written for the National Tea Party Convention in Nashville, Carender identified her influences as writers and philosophers like Thomas Sowell and Thomas Jefferson, Ayn Rand and William F. Buckley, Frederic Bastiat and Milton Friedman. Discussing health care, she later said she believed that it should be more based in charity—on voluntary transactions rather than raising taxes to subsidize it, or requiring it of all citizens.

She had continued to do rallies. Sally Oljar, a graphic designer in her fifties who had offered to help after the first event, now ran Seattle Sons and Daughters of Liberty with her and had become a national coordinator for Tea Party Patriots, connecting Carender to the national network. But in her second year as a Tea Party activist, Carender, now thirty, decided to begin working on local issues. After the rally in Olympia, she entered the marble labyrinth of the state capitol to try to find her representatives. The legislature had just suspended a measure passed by citizen initiative that had required a two-thirds supermajority for tax increases. Lawmakers were dealing with the same kind of budget crisis that was plaguing state governments across the country. But Carender thought they had not done enough to cut spending before raising taxes. She knew, though, that she was waging an uphill battle; her representatives reflected Seattle's mostly liberal voters.

As she walked into the first office, she met only an aide. They spoke across a low desk partition, but it may as well have been a high brick wall.

"We don't want to affect the neediest, we don't want to affect police or fire or things like that," Carender said. "We want to cut the unnecessary things. And it seems to me, as a taxpayer, that all the options for cutting things have not happened at all, including reopening the contracts for state employees and their pensions and benefits and all that stuff."

As the aide listened, Carender continued her bill of particulars. "When a private employee gets laid off, they don't go to the top of some other list to get hired onto some other state job; they don't get these incredible benefits," she said. "It just, it feels like a knife in my heart when I know that I have to pay more revenue to pay somebody else's salary and somebody else's benefits. It's not me going into a store and having a voluntary transaction with someone where we both benefit. What I want to see is, before coming to us for more money we don't have, and taking away jobs from the private sector, make these cuts."

The aide continued to nod silently. Carender thought for a moment, finger to mouth, "Oh, one more thing, a personal story," she said. "I would like to start my own business. I would like to open a café." But, she explained, she feared all the taxes: income tax, payroll tax, unemployment tax. "All those things that I know, because I have friends that are business owners, all these things are going up on them."

"I can't believe this is the America that I grew up in as a kid," she went on. "Because to me, it was always like it didn't matter what you wanted to do, you could do it if you put in the work. Now I'm at the place in my life where I'm like, maybe I can't do that because it's not going to be successful. It's not going to be worth the work to get around how much the state is trying to tax me. And it's really, like, a depressing feeling. It's a really depressing feeling."

The aide agreed that it was scary to start a new business. But lots of people do succeed, she said. Cheerfully, she suggested Carender look into programs the state offered to help minorities and women open businesses.

Carender looked as if she might erupt. "I'm the type of person who would want to do that myself," she said.

"I know, but you say the state of Washington is not helping," the aide said.

"I'm not asking for help," Carender countered. "I'm asking for you guys to stay out of my way. I'm asking for you to get out of the way so I can do my own thing, start a business and not have to worry about these various things I'm going to have to pay for."

"Dealing with taxes comes with owning a business," the aide said.

"It doesn't necessarily have to," Carender replied. "Every small business owner will tell you, the only thing they want is for government to get out of the way. I just, I just basically want the government to shrink and I want my tax dollars back and I want to live my life without the government intruding on every part of it, which it seems like it's doing."

The aide was silent again, and Carender turned to go. "Thank you for listening," she said.

The aide in the second office was more encouraging, urging Carender to email her boss ("and cc me") a report Carender had cited that identified where the state could cut waste. But the aide also pointed out that only 33 percent of the legislator's constituents had voted for the initiative requiring a supermajority to raise taxes, so her vote to suspend it was not ignoring the will of her voters.

"She's right," Carender reflected, resigned, as she walked out. "What do you do?" Then she brightened. "Actually, what you do, you start talking to your neighbors and start convincing them to think like you do."

She went outside to look for some friends, a group of fellow conservatives she met through Young Republicans. As she crossed the capitol grounds, she saw that the antitax rally had given way to an opposing demonstration, this one against budget cuts. A protester offered Carender a handout arguing against cuts to education.

"I actually support budget cuts, but thanks," she said. She snatched the handout, then winked.

꙳

Diana Reimer came to the movement more through circumstance.

The daughter of a Democratic committeeman in Philadelphia, she dropped out of high school in the tenth grade and worked in the bar her father ran. She married Don when he was still in the Navy, then they and their two children moved to the suburbs.

The Reimers had refinanced their house in 2005 with an interest-only loan. The mortgage broker had told them they would avoid the steep increase in the rate if they weren't planning to be in the house more than ten years. That fit with their plans. Their children had grown, and they were eager to move back to South Philadelphia, "where our son is, and where Don could get some exercise," Diana said, looking kindly at her barrel-chested husband seated next to her on the couch.

They put the house on the market in the summer of 2008, but months later it had not sold, and the real estate agent told them it would only sell for less than the amount they owed on their mortgage. Worried that Don would lose his job as a technician for an insurance company, Diana had started working at Macy's for $7.65 an hour, even though she had worked for ten years at Strawbridge's, in Philadelphia, for a higher wage. A few months later, the inevitable happened. Don was given a choice: retire or be fired.

Anxious about the house and their debt, Diana saw a story about the Tea Party on Fox News in March 2009. A quick web search turned up the group Tax Day Tea Party, the precursor to Tea Party Patriots. Diana signed on to be the coordinator of the Tea Party in Philadelphia, setting up a Facebook account and planning an event, just as the how-to list instructed.

"It wasn't a political thing," she said. "It was a way to get out there and get your frustrations out. Holding a sign and cheering and saying the Pledge of Allegiance."

While she was at work, Don drove to Philadelphia to get a permit for the event in Love Park. They were thinking big, they wanted a sound system. A clerk told Don that this would require electricity and technicians, and that they would have to pay $8,000 for a permit. Don drove home and told his wife they couldn't do it.

"Oh yes we can," she replied. "People are depending on us."

"That's my gal," Don said, smiling as he recounted the story. "That's when I became a believer."

She called Tax Day Tea Party, which put out an email alert to its membership that she needed help. Tea Party callers then deluged the Philadelphia parks department demanding that the Reimers not have to pay a fee. It turned out to be something of a misunderstanding; as long as they were willing to bring their own generator and sound system, it would still qualify as a political demonstration, and there would be no fee. Indicating how fast the movement's rancor was spreading, calls continued to clog the parks department phones even after Diana put out the word that the problem had been solved; people on the Tax Day email list had forwarded the alert to other Tea Party email lists. "I had no idea how it would mushroom," she said.

Soon the Reimers were holding a July 4 Tea Party, a march on the state capitol in Harrisburg, and getting people to crowd the town hall where Arlen Specter was shouted down.

By September, Diana had completed FreedomWorks training and was speaking at the 9/12 march.

She was doing her Tea Party Patriots conference call Monday nights, and her state coalition call Tuesdays. She was taking her laptop and her lunch to work so she could find a quiet corner of the mall to keep up with Tea Party matters. Finally, when Don found her up late one night answering emails, he suggested she take a sabbatical from work. When Macy's did not allow it, he encouraged her to quit.

"That's how strongly I believe in what we're doing, what she's doing," he said. "She needs to concentrate on this. She does this very well, she's an inspiration to people."

Diana loved the solidarity. "It's amazing to see the American people coming together just like a big family," she said. "It just overwhelms you. They're there, they come from all over, they're all there for the same purpose."

It was the same sense of community that she and her husband remembered from growing up in South Philadelphia, a feeling they had not been able to find elsewhere.

"The neighborhoods were different, the values aren't as well honored today," Don said. "People would talk to their neighbors, have block parties, there was less stress in life. An elderly man would holler at the kids, we'd listen because he was an adult. Today they come right in your face."

"We know about four neighbors," he said, gesturing at the suburban street outside. "We've been here nineteen years."

A warm, exuberant woman, Diana brought enthusiasm to whatever she did. Exploring her family roots in the Abruzzo region of Italy, she had met some locals who ran tours of the area, and she and Don began helping to promote and run them until 9/11 made travel difficult. She had immersed herself in photography, elaborately framing photographs she had

taken on their travels. But she had not been particularly political before 2009. Talking about Barack Obama's presidential
campaign, which had lavished attention on Pennsylvania, she
said, "I thought he was just supposed to be some congressman."

"Senator," Don corrected her.

"He was a senator?" Diana said. She laughed it off. Don
was the bigger reader, she pointed out. "I'm better at doing.
Phone calls, talking, getting people motivated."

As the Tea Party grew, there were more and more recruits like
Diana Reimer. Their ideology, if they had one, was evolving,
and so it could be inconsistent and contradictory; the famous
comment, "Keep your government hands off my Medicare,"
at a town hall in South Carolina was ridiculed as evidence of
the stupidity of the movement. But it mostly reflected frustration. The country was awash in massive problems, and it was
easy to believe that the government was in the way of a
solution. The Tea Partiers who argued for fiscal responsibility
didn't focus on the details—like the fact that any meaningful
cuts in the deficit would require deep cuts in programs that
most Americans, and most Tea Partiers, supported: the military, Medicare.

While younger Tea Partiers like Keli Carender started with
the ideology and became more practical, older ones like Diana
Reimer became more ideological over time. Freedom became
more than just a patriotic idea you promoted by saying the
Pledge of Allegiance at a meeting.

As Congress began debating health care reform legislation, Diana was concerned mostly about cuts to Medicare and
Tricare, benefits that she and Don liked. "I don't care what

they say—'There's no death squads.' Maybe that's a bad name for it," she said. "But why do they want to keep the elderly around when they have the young people? Where are they going to make these cuts?"

"Government was put here for certain reasons," she added, "they were not put here to run banks, insurance companies, and health care, and automobile companies. They were put here to keep us safe."

A few days later, she acknowledged that Medicare was a government program.

"It's also going bankrupt," she said. "This is what the government does, they run things, they run it into the ground." But she had few answers as to how to fix it. "That's not my job to figure it out," she said. "Someone has got to figure out how to reform it and reform it right but not—just fix what's broken."

She was clearly irked by liberals who thought the Tea Partiers were hypocritical. As Congress debated the health care bill, she joined other Tea Partiers in a protest at George Mason University in Virginia, where President Obama was delivering a speech. They had met some students demonstrating in support of the health care legislation. "You know, I'm going to read up on Social Security and Medicare," she said afterward. "Because as soon as they see me coming, that's what they say, 'Well, you're on Medicare, that's a government program.' And I'm getting sick of it. Talk about the issues, not me. I had to go on Medicare, and Social Security is my right. Especially, what—these twenty-year-old suits?"

And she did hone her arguments. She felt that the students supporting health care reform were the ones who were not recognizing reality. "To them," she said later, "the government is going to take care of us, now we don't have to worry about it. That's not America." America, she believed, was a land of entrepreneurs. She had started working when she was just fourteen, at a gift shop on Germantown Avenue in Philadelphia. If Medicare and Social Security didn't exist, she said, "I'd find something else and that would be my choice." Big government wanted to rob the country of that independent spirit. "They like to take that all away so you don't have to be creative," she said. "And I'm a creative person."

She had been open to persuasion about her politics before. When Ronald Reagan was running for president in 1980, a neighbor in Virginia Beach, where she and Don were living during his final stint in the Navy, came over and asked them who they were going to vote for. They had been brought up as Democrats, so they said Jimmy Carter. The neighbor explained why they shouldn't. Years later, Diana couldn't remember what the neighbor said, but she remembered that he was convincing enough that she and Don changed their registration and voted for Reagan. They had been Republicans ever since.

Now she believed she might be able to change minds herself. As frustrated as she had been that day at George Mason, she was heartened a few weeks later when a young man she had met there called and said he was going to start a Tea Party on campus.

"I gave him my card," she said. "If I had anything to do with that, I'm very happy."

⌇

By the weekend of March 20, when the House was scheduled to vote on the health care bill, demonstrators on both sides of the issue had swarmed the Capitol.

There were lines out the office doors of the few legislators

who had not yet announced how they would vote. Tea Partiers filled the galleries above the House floor and the under-
ground tunnels of the House office buildings to buttonhole
lawmakers on their way to vote. Outside, they held candle-
light vigils.

Diana Reimer and Brendan Steinhauser were distributing
the FreedomWorks packets with a letter from Dick Armey
("Dear Friend of Freedom, Thank you for being in Washington during this critical hour of the struggle to prevent a government takeover of the American health care system") and a
list of dos and don'ts for lobbying. Arrive five minutes early,
it suggested, be specific about how the legislation will affect
you, always be polite. "You will never convince your lawmaker
or their staff with rudeness, vulgarity, or threats," the Tea Partiers were advised.

Given the emotions that had been building, it was inevi-
table that this last admonition would be ignored. Glenn Beck
was comparing the health care legislation to Pearl Harbor or
the Civil War. John Boehner, the House Republican minority
leader, warned of "Armageddon" if the bill passed. After the
vote was announced, Representative Steve King rallied Tea
Partiers outside the Capitol. "Let's beat the other side to a
pulp!" he shouted. "Let's chase them down! There's going to
be a reckoning!"

And worse. Representative John Lewis of Georgia, the
House's most visible hero of the civil rights movement, told
reporters that he had been called "nigger" as he was leaving
the Cannon House Office Building. Emanuel Cleaver, a black
congressman from Maryland, said that he had been spat on by
protesters as he walked behind Lewis. Another protester called
Barney Frank a "homo" as he walked between the House
buildings.

The Tea Partiers had been talking about their cause using the language of the civil rights movement, comparing themselves to the Freedom Riders. Now that lawmakers who were actual veterans of that movement were accusing them of such hatefulness, many Tea Partiers refused to believe it was true. Rather than explain it as a fringe of the movement, which they plausibly might have, they argued that the ugliness had never happened. Wasn't it suspicious, they asked, that there was no video of spitting or slurs, in an age when everyone's cell phone has a camera?

It was difficult, if not disingenuous, for the Tea Party groups to try to disown the behavior. They had organized the rally, and under their model of self-policing, they were responsible for the behavior of people who were there. And after saying for months that anybody could be a Tea Party leader, they could not suddenly dismiss as faux Tea Partiers those protesters who made them look bad. To pretend that the sentiments did not exist was to ignore the most noxious signs that had been showing up at rallies for a year. Some activists, like Jennifer Stefano, recognized that the Tea Party had to acknowledge what had happened and repudiate it. She issued a statement declaring that "Under no circumstance should any Tea Party group give bigotry cover."

"I am sorry this incident happened," she wrote, "Not just because Congressman Lewis and the others who were targeted did not deserve it, but those within the Tea Party movement who are legitimately fighting for their beliefs did not deserve to be sullied by a few ignorant people."

A statement from Tea Party Patriots did not go so far as to apologize; it noted that the organization had a "zero tolerance policy" against violence or bigotry and expected "this standard to be applied to all."

"By the same token," the statement added, "public anger at Congress is legitimate and warranted."

They were right about one thing: the ugliness did come from both sides.

"Fuck you," began one email that Diana Reimer opened up as she arrived home after this trip to Washington. "You tea baggers are the most insolent uneducated, and just plain STUPID rednecks. You should all be euthanized. Or maybe just given the bubonic plague. Then tell me you don't want free healthcare for all. Stop buying into capitalism. I only WISH Barack Obama was a socialist, then we'd have real policies that focus on PEOPLE not on the fucking economy. JUST STOP. PLEASE. YOU MAKE AMERICANS LOOK LIKE IDIOTS IN THE INTER-NATIONAL COMMUNITY."

"These people are cowards," Diana said. She hadn't seen any of the insults directed at the Democratic congressmen. Instead, she recalled the protests fondly. "We were out there chanting, 'We'll remember in November,' 'One term presi-dent,' 'Kill the bill!' "

Don, who had joined her for the weekend, had shaken the hand of the actor Jon Voight, who was there in Washington with the Tea Party Express. "I thanked him for coming out for the values of this country," he said. "It was a real honor."

Diana took heart from another email. "While I have not met you personally, I certainly always keep my ears and eyes open in case I hear your name at an event, as I would be hon-ored to meet you some day," the writer said. "I can't tell you how proud I am to be an American."

"That's what I don't understand," Diana said. "It's impor-tant to so many people. How can they not see? It's not just me and Don. We had fifty thousand people there. Doesn't that mean anything?"

But she was not discouraged by the bill's passage. There was a rumor that Mark Levin, the conservative radio talk show host, would file a lawsuit against the new health care law, and the attorneys general of several states were planning to file lawsuits as well.

"I had one second when I felt depressed," she said. "Then I said"—she clapped her hands—"now the work begins."

CHAPTER EIGHT

"We've been a little bit too nice"

At its heart, the Tea Party movement was deeply divided. The people who held virulent signs at rallies were a very different group from those who sat through meetings about organizing local precincts, who in turn were different from those who stayed home but sympathized with the cause. Younger Tea Partiers extolling the wisdom of Friedrich Hayek and Ludwig von Mises had different priorities from the older Tea Partiers who wanted change but also wanted their Medicare left alone. Even the movement's harshest critics acknowledged a kind of "good Tea Party" / "bad Tea Party" divide. The liberal group Media Matters for America had devoted a great deal of time and effort to tracking the Fox News Channel's promotion of the Tea Parties and debunking the movement's received wisdom, but when it sent a researcher undercover to the Tea Party Convention in Nashville, she reported back how "affable and welcoming" her fellow conventioneers were. "A nice surprise was the lack of violent language," wrote the researcher, Melinda Warner, who described herself as an evangelical conservative-turned-progressive. "The members who make those horrible signs and make violent and hateful comments either were not in attendance or kept their mouths shut and left their signs at home."

They were, of course, all part of the whole. As it entered its second year, the Tea Party movement had become a mirror as well as a magnet: it reflected back whatever its individual members wanted to project onto it. To some Tea Partiers it was a vessel for grievance, inchoate or specific. To others it was a means to electoral victory against the Democrats. Libertarians hoped it would force the Republican Party to fight more for fiscal discipline, while constitutional purists hoped it would cleanse the country of its New Deal–Great Society sins. The Tea Party was like the proverbial blind men and the elephant; it had a different shape and texture depending on what was in front of you.

Even people within the movement were not always clear about its goals. Tea Party Patriots, which, as an umbrella of more than two thousand local Tea Party groups, best reflected the grassroots origins of the movement, declared as its motto, "Limited government, fiscal responsibility, and free markets." This was in line with the priorities advocated by FreedomWorks and by those who promoted libertarian philosophy. Most local groups embraced some version of this motto, saying they wanted to focus on fiscal problems and not divisive social issues like abortion or gay marriage or immigration. "Every social issue you bring in, you're adding planks to your mission," said Frank Anderson, a founder of the Independence Caucus, which worked with Tea Party groups to evaluate candidates' positions on issues. "And planks become splinters." Yet as Tea Party Patriots invited people to submit ideas for the Contract from America, which was the closest thing to a manifesto of what the Tea Party movement wanted Congress to do, among the more popular suggestions were "an official language of the United States" and "amend the Endangered Species Act." (Another proposal: "Legalize hemp.") Any armchair originalist could tell you that these were not among the powers enumerated in the Constitution.

And if some goals championed by Tea Partiers weren't envisioned by the more purist strains of the movement, others directly contradicted it. Wendy Day, a leader of the Michigan Tea Party, told an interviewer that one good use of government would be to "force credit card companies to lower interest rates for everyone." Jeff McQueen, the creator of the Tea Party flag, had been laid off from his job in international sales for an auto parts company, and he argued that the government had pushed him into unemployment because it had failed to promote American car companies. McQueen pointed out that in Japan and Korea, government policy forced everyone to drive cars manufactured there.

Most Tea Partiers did not see themselves as racists, and you could go to their meetings and get not get a whiff of racist attitudes. But with its talk of states' rights and protecting what was rightfully yours, the movement was inherently attractive to people who believed that the government had coddled minorities and the disadvantaged. Along a rural stretch of road near Akron, Ohio, the resident of a ranch house that was well maintained and decorated with more than a dozen American flags displayed a Tea Party manifesto in six precisely placed lawn signs:

YOU ARE ENTERING THE ZONE OF A VAST RIGHT-WING
    CONSPIRACY
WE ARE FOR THE TEA PARTY, GUNS, GOD AND LIFE

IMPEACH OBAMA

THE USA NEEDS A FRESH, LIGHT PAINT JOB

TRICKLE UP SOCIALISM AT WORK

YOU ARE NOW LEAVING THE ZONE OF A VAST RIGHT-WING
    CONSPIRACY

The rallies themselves best captured the scrum of interests competing for attention. They were a mix of the committed, the curious, and the cantankerous (and sometimes, the crazy). But just as important were the people who had never been to a rally but supported the movement from afar. "For every one of us, there's two or three hundred at home," said Bob Glover, a chemist for the U.S. Customs Service who had come from Savannah, Georgia, to a rally in Washington, D.C. Even if Glover's guess overstated the numbers, there was fertile ground among ordinary Americans for the Tea Party's arguments. You couldn't ignore the rallies. But you had to listen to the folks at home, too, because they represented the growth potential for the Tea Party. It was striking how many people came out for their first demonstrations in the spring of 2010, even as those activists who had started the movement had begun to tire of the public spectacles. Both groups would be voting for Tea Party candidates. And both groups revealed different things about the free-floating discontent in the land.

~

Thousands of Tea Party tourists descended on the Mojave Desert town of Searchlight, Nevada, population 532, on Saturday, March 27, the weekend after the House passed the health care bill. The Tea Party Express was kicking off its third cross-country bus tour, and organizers had billed the event as the "Showdown in Searchlight," the Tea Party versus Harry

Reid, the leader of the Senate's Democratic majority. For a week, a small fleet of bulldozers and dump trucks had been grading about twenty acres of rolling desert just outside of town to create a site for the rally. In town, there wasn't much to see; its main attractions were the elementary school named for Reid and the Nugget casino, a less glitzy version of its Las Vegas competitors that might have been mistaken for a highway rest stop. Next door loomed a new billboard invoking a Democratic icon from the Great Depression to tweak the hometown senator: WILL ROGERS NEVER MET HARRY REID.

The license plates on the cars streaming into town on U.S. Route 95 made clear that a good chunk of the crowd would not be able to cast a vote for or against Harry Reid—a fact the senator noted in a press release encouraging the visitors to spend their out-of-state dollars to boost Nevada's hard-hit economy. Voting, for today, was beside the point. "After the crap they pulled, the federal government, we had to show up," said Don Francis, a retired vice president at a corporate recruiting firm. "There was no way we were not going to show up."

He and his wife, Shirl, had come in from Orange County, California, and had been lucky to score a room at the El Rey Motel—nothing much, but unbeatable for proximity to the rally. They and another couple who had driven in with them had wandered the parking lot the night before the rally in their UCLA sweatshirts, carrying Seabreezes (vodka with cranberry and grapefruit juices) in go-cups. They had never been to a Tea Party rally before, but they were angry about health care. It would bankrupt the federal government and burden small businesses, Francis said. He hated the sweetheart deals that had been brokered to get the bill passed, and he was convinced that the new law would provide government health insurance to illegal immigrants. The reality was

that the nonpartisan Congressional Budget Office had calcu-
lated that the plan would actually reduce the deficit, and the
legislation explicitly blocked illegal immigrants from the public health care exchanges. Francis wasn't buying it. "How
many times has Obama stood up and lied?" he said. "He said
it was all going to happen in open session on—what's the TV
station?—C-Span."

He and his wife had come to Searchlight, he said, "because
it's nearby, it's timely, and we felt it was appropriate. I'm not a
political activist. I'm a sixty-six-year-old American who's fed
up with the state government and the federal government."

Jeff Church had driven five hundred miles from Reno with
a "Reject Reid" bumper sticker pasted on his hybrid. "If they
printed one saying 'Reject Ensign,' I'd have that, too," he
said, referring to the state's other U.S. senator, a Republican
who had spent much of the last year battling charges that he
had had an affair with a staff member and then tried to pay off
her husband by securing him a job. Church, a retired police
officer and a trainer for police recruiters, had been to just one
Tea Party event before. He had voted for Ross Perot in 1992,
and he was most angry about government spending. "I don't
mean to insult drunken sailors, but at least drunken sailors,
when they run out of money, they stop spending."

Where was Congress, he asked, when the economy was
melting down? "Why weren't they standing on the table
screaming, 'The banks are out of control!' Don't loan money
to people who can't pay it back. There should have been regulations." A call for more bank regulation was not part of the
free-market Tea Party message, but Church yearned for the
days of bipartisan problem solving. "Why can't they get along
together and make some common-sense solutions?" he asked.

The Tea Party Express had hired Sarah Palin to speak at

the rally in Searchlight, and all week television stations had
been predicting gridlock on the only road in and out of town.
Recreational vehicles began winding down the dirt road to
the newly cleared rally site the night before, and people set
bonfires to keep warm overnight against the high desert winds.
Cars started pouring in as soon as the gates opened on Saturday morning at six A.M. SUVs with California plates had messages scrawled on their back windshields: "OVERTAXED!"
read one, while another proclaimed, "Defend the Constitution! Going to Tea Party Express, Searchlight, Nevada."

With bright sunshine interrupted by sharp bursts of a dust
storm, people huddled under blankets in their lawn chairs with
their children and portable coffee makers, or trekked with their
"Don't Tread on Me" flags up the hills studded with Joshua
Trees. Someone had set up a face-off between a Lamborghini
("capitalism") and a Yugo ("socialism.") Food trucks did a brisk
business near the entrance.

LIAR, THUG, TRAITOR, COMMIE USURPER, read one woman's
placard, next to a picture of President Obama as the devil. KARL
MARX AND MAO WERE NOT FOUNDING FATHERS, read another.
There was another sign with Obama's face superimposed on a
picture of a Papua New Guinean, identifying him as your new
doctor under the just-passed health care legislation. And others: WHY WON'T HE SHOW US HIS PAPERS? STOP GLOBAL WHINING.
Members of Oath Keepers, the group made up of military and
law enforcement personnel who pledged not to enforce any
federal order they considered unconstitutional, held up a large
banner for their organization.

Kim Lefner, a Californian in her fifties, was wearing a Los
Angeles Angels sun visor and carrying a clutch of cardboard
pitchforks and torches. "You can't bring real pitchforks, so
these just make a statement," she said. Not that she wouldn't

like the real kind. "We've been a little bit too nice," said her friend Nancy Davey.

Lefner had started making the pitchforks and torches (ten dollars a set) the previous summer after the first Tea Party rallies. "It's capitalism at its finest," she said. "Seeing a need and filling a passion." She belonged to the Orange County chapter of As a Mom, Glenn Beck's group for women, which she said was focused mainly on educating people about the Constitution. "My kids are grown," she explained, "I have time to put into changing things that I don't like." The women had driven 260 miles to Searchlight because they were angry about health care. "They didn't hear us," Davey said. "It was not representative government. They're trying to insert government into every area of our lives." Lefner had looked around Harry Reid's small hometown and hadn't thought much of it. "The houses are falling apart," she said. "Could he not send a few dollars their way?"

Basil and Kathryn Kelly had driven even farther—1,100 miles from their filbert farm in Aurora, Oregon. "It's always been the progressive movement chipping away at our freedoms. Now it is a full frontal attack," Basil said. "On health care, for the first time in my life I'm seeing Congress move in the exact opposite way than people are asking."

The newly passed health care legislation was the immediate spark for many protesters. A Revolutionary War reenactor ascended a metal stage and read a bill of particulars against "the liberals." "They defile the Constitution with the health care bill and will force the people to buy something," he proclaimed in period accent.

Reflecting the proximity to the Mexican border, just 250 miles to the south, many had come out to express their anger about immigration. "It's overwhelming our schools, our neighborhoods," said John Roddy, who had driven with his wife, Shirley, from San Diego. "Our neighborhoods are being overrun by multiple families in houses." The Roddys said they had nothing against helping the needy. "But if we do, they don't put forth the effort," Shirley said. "We've given them so much they don't help themselves."

There were a few candidates working the crowd, including Republicans seeking the party's nomination to face Reid in the November general election. Danny Tarkanian, a son of the legendary college basketball coach Jerry Tarkanian (who had won a national championship in 1990 at the University of Nevada, Las Vegas) looked out of place as he stiffly shook hands wearing a blue blazer and gray flannel slacks. Sharron Angle, another frontrunner, was more in the spirit, arriving on a Harley-Davidson motorcycle and wearing a leather biker jacket as she threw her arm around Tea Partiers to pose for pictures.

Foreign camera crews roamed the crowd trying to make sense of this American phenomenon. In the back, a woman paced in front of a bank of television cameras screaming, "You're so slanted! You make me sick! Are you going to tell the truth?"

What made someone come out for this kind of spectacle, and what made someone watching from home support it? The *New York Times*/CBS News poll offered some hints, if you compared the people who supported the movement with the smaller group of people who were activists. The supporters were angry, but the activists were angrier. They disapproved of both President Obama and the Republican Party more intensely. They believed more fervently that the president did not share the values that most Americans try to live by. They were more likely to say that the bank bailout had been unnecessary, and that they had no confidence in the Federal Reserve as a steward of the American economy. Supporters, meanwhile, didn't know much about the Federal Reserve, or about Ron Paul, who had been railing against it for decades and whose supporters had made "Audit the Fed!" a rallying cry for Tea Partiers. And while supporters were more inclined to blame Wall Street for the failure of the economy, the activists blamed Congress. Supporters thought the government should focus on reducing the deficit, the activists wanted to cut taxes—not surprising given that they were also more likely to say that their taxes were unfair. And the activists took a harder line on reducing the size of government, saying they supported doing so even if it meant cutting Social Security, Medicare, education, and defense spending.

But the two groups shared an underlying suspicion of the government and other institutions, as well as a deep belief that the country was on the wrong track. In interviews with supporters, the same words came up and again. Some of them were straight off Glenn Beck's chalkboard diagrams about the evils of progressivism: Obama was a Marxist. He had associated with violent sixties radicals. He had stuffed the government with "czars" too corrupt to pass Senate confirmation. And his administration was trying to bring about a crisis so that it could swoop in with more government control—after all, Rahm Emanuel, the president's chief of staff, had said, "You never want a serious crisis to go to waste."

But more than that, those who supported the Tea Party movement talked about the arrogance of power in Washington. Like the most active Tea Partiers, they believed that the country had moved away from the Constitution and that the

Republican Party had moved away from conservative values. People wanted to clean house in Congress. Then again, they also complained that change was coming dangerously fast. What bothered them most was a sense that they and their concerns were being disregarded. It was clear that those attending Tea Party rallies were not the only ones with a vague, often contradictory sense that something was just wrong in America.

"I support the Tea Party because they are saying we the people are taking back the country. We have gotten away from we the people," said Dee Close, a forty-seven-year-old homemaker in Memphis, Tennessee, in a follow-up interview to the *Times* poll. "When Republicans as well as Democrats get to Washington, they get caught up in using strategy, and they don't have the backbone to fight for what they stand for."

Richard Harris, a sixty-one-year-old truck driver in Florida, went even further. "I see less and less need for government," he said. "They call themselves my representatives, but basically they don't represent me."

Distrust was a recurring theme for those Americans sympathetic to the Tea Party, and government was merely at the top of the list of the institutions they distrusted. For all the activists' rhetoric of letting the free market work, many Tea Party supporters were not prepared to give the financial industry a pass. "The system is broken," said Richard Gilbert, a retired teacher in Aiken, South Carolina. "I think Obama has potential but we don't want to be like Europe. Nothing can be accomplished until we get rid of the current mess and until there is some way of controlling Wall Street."

Many people looked at the Tea Parties and did not see monsters; they saw Americans taking care of a need. "The Tea Party, they're just everybody," said Martha McKenzie, an eighty-four-year-old Republican voter in Bowling Green, Kentucky, who saw the Tea Party as "well-organized people, getting the word out. They're just average Americans with the courage to disagree."

When Democracy Corps, the political research firm founded by the Democratic strategists James Carville and Stanley Greenberg, convened focus groups among conservatives in the fall of 2009, they heard the same sentiments expressed.

The participants celebrated the Tea Parties even though they had not been to any rallies themselves, and they were frustrated with the mainstream news organizations, who they felt portrayed the Tea Partiers as crazy. "You know, you are all nut jobs out there holding Tea Parties," said one person, mockingly. "But at least they were showing that something was going on. I mean, we are ignored. I didn't attend a Tea Party but we, the people, were nonexistent according to some of the news stations."

Asked what they wanted, or what they believed the Tea Party movement wanted, the focus group participants expressed a common refrain about returning the country to its founding values as expressed in the Constitution—though they did not agree on what that meant.

"I don't want big government," one participant said. "I want the people to have the say-so."

Another offered: "I want to get back to the principles on which we were founded, the principles that say, In God We Trust, which is written above in that, in the House, what do you call it, the Speaker's House, is that where it is? I forget where it is. Anyway, In God We Trust."

The fact that the Tea Party was so many different things to so many different people—if they knew exactly what it was, at all—was threatening to work against it in many places. When it came to elections, local Tea Party groups knew they had to avoid splitting their vote, and so they often tried to unite behind a single candidate in Republican primaries where there were often many self-described Tea Party candidates on the ballot. In the Fifth District of Virginia, Tea Party groups issued "Lump Reports," awarding congressional candidates "lumps of sugar" for traits that would make them strong contenders: their ability to raise money, their appeal to grassroots groups, their adherence to Tea Party values. The groups pledged to support the candidate with the most lumps, or, as they described it, "The more lumps, the sweeter the Tea."

In Nevada, Tea Party leaders were hoping to unite groups behind a single Republican candidate to challenge Harry Reid, but there were twelve people running in the Republican primary, and none was attracting a majority of Tea Party support. Some Tea Partiers considered Bill Parson, a former Marine and project manager at the Nevada nuclear test site, the purest because he was not a politician. But others thought that Sharron Angle, a former state assemblywoman, might be a more pragmatic choice. And then there was Danny Tarkanian, who had name recognition because of his father. Sue Lowden was also a familiar name to many voters. She was a former state Republican Party chairwoman, but she had clashed with libertarian activists two years earlier over her refusal to certify convention delegates for Ron Paul in the 2008 presidential race. (Paul had done better in Nevada than anywhere else, but the party establishment had lined up behind John McCain.)

There was also the problem of Scott Ashjian, a former asphalt contractor who filed papers to establish an official Tea Party line on the Nevada ballot and run as its candidate in November. Leaders of local Tea Parties insisted that he had never been to a single Tea Party event and suggested that he was a "progressive plant" put up by liberals to take votes away from the eventual Republican candidate and reelect Reid. (Reid had won in the past by less than a majority, thanks to the presence of multiple candidates on the ballot.) A poll by the *Las Vegas Review-Journal* showed that a generic Tea Party candidate running on a third-party line would indeed split the vote and allow Reid to win. So Tea Party leaders felt compelled to announce that the Tea Partiers in Nevada would no longer be calling themselves the Tea Party—the new preferred term would be "grassroots." They sued (unsuccessfully) to get Ashjian bounced from the ballot. And a local prosecutor who happened to be a former state Republican chairman filed charges against him for bouncing a $5,000 check, though the prosecutor denied there were any politics involved. (The charges were dismissed.) The political action committee behind the Tea Party Express, whose money had helped Scott Brown defeat Martha Coakley in Massachusetts and which had already spent about $500,000 in the race against Reid, took out a television ad against Ashjian with a message from the "real" Tea Party groups: Get Lost. "None of us has ever heard of you," Mark Williams, the chairman of the Tea Party Express, scolded.

Debbie Landis, the leader of Anger Is Brewing, another Nevada Tea Party group, took the stage at the March 27 rally in Searchlight and announced that her group and more than a dozen others had signed a statement opposing this new Tea Party on the ballot: "Which never has been and never will be affiliated with the grassroots effort in Nevada." But the crowd, later estimated at seven thousand people, began to thin after Sarah Palin spoke. That left relatively few people at the Showdown in Searchlight to hear from the most prominent candidates seeking to face Reid. The Tea Party tourists had another engagement to rush off to—the Tea Party Express had departed for a later rally in nearby Henderson, where the special guest would be a conservative favorite, Ann Coulter.

~

The Tea Party Express was winding its bus tour toward Washington for Tax Day on April 15, which had become a high holiday for the movement. The day before, the caravan stopped in Boston, the symbolic home of the Tea Partiers and the site of their biggest victory so far. Sarah Palin spoke again there. Scott Brown, notably, stayed away.

Some Tea Partiers disdained the Tea Party Express as "The Astroturf Express," because it was run by Republican consultants. But the object for Tax Day was to make a big splash, so it was everyone in the pool. FreedomWorks and the Tea Party Express were working together in planning the event, joined by longstanding conservative advocacy groups like Americans for Tax Reform and the American Conservative Union.

A year in, many Americans were still confused about what the Tea Party movement was all about. FreedomWorks held its "Liberty Summit" at the Ronald Reagan Building to train would-be activists in organizing and getting out the vote. People streamed in carrying "Don't Tread on Me" flags, until a guard supervising the metal detector at the door announced to her colleagues that no more flags would be allowed in.

"American flags?" asked a man working the machine.

"The American flag has stripes, stars," the supervisor said. "That flag had a snake on it; it said Don't Tread Me or something."

She then refined her rule: "No flags with words on them."

In the lobby, women wearing the signature fuchsia of the left-wing protest group Code Pink were walking around with questionnaires, trying to understand the motivations of the Tea Partiers. They were making Matt Kibbe and Brendan Steinhauser of FreedomWorks nervous, but some of the women pronounced themselves impressed. "It's rational talk, for the most part," said one Code Pink activist, Joan Stallard. "It's strategizing. I agree; if you want something done, you have to go to the precincts."

Inside the summit, Lord Monckton, a British global warming denier, posed for photographs with Tea Partiers carrying Jeff McQueen's flag of the Second American Revolution. Young representatives from antitax groups encouraged the Tea Partiers to get involved locally to fight property tax assessments. Led by Dick Armey, the Tea Partiers went across Pennsylvania Avenue to join the cacophony of the rally in Freedom Plaza. Steve King was onstage, declaring, "We do not believe in a government that's oppressive, nor do we believe in a government that confiscates our earnings and rewards people that don't earn, and eats our substance and drains American vitality. That's what's going on in America today.

"Cars," he added, "should be made by Americans."

A sign read:

THE COMPANY I WORKED FOR DOWNSIZED AND LAID ME OFF TO SAVE MONEY. I THINK IT'S TIME TO DOWNSIZE THE GOVERNMENT AND SAVE US MONEY.

Another quoted Bastiat's *The Law* on legal plunder:

THE LAW TAKES FROM SOME PERSON WHAT BELONGS TO THEM AND GIVES TO ANOTHER PERSON TO WHOM IT DOES NOT BELONG!

A white flag featured the silhouette of a gun, with the legend "Come Ahead and Take It."

As the crowds gathered again that evening for the Freedom-Works rally under the Washington Monument, the show was a blend of jingoism and grievance. Lord Monckton declared America the land of opportunity: "You can be born in Kenya and end up as president of the United States!" He led the crowd in cheers of "Global warming is bullshit!" and urged people to scream loud enough that the White House could hear. "Albert Arnold Gore," he declared gleefully, "I am coming to get you!" Victoria Jackson, the former *Saturday Night Live* star, sang "There's a Communist in the White House" again, with her ukelele. And a group of coal miners from a West Virginia mine where twenty-nine people had died a week earlier ascended the stage, wearing their helmets, to complain that cap-and-trade would devastate their industry by raising energy prices and driving out jobs. SENATORS, DON'T SEND OUR JOBS TO ASIA, read one of their signs. "We're tired of hearing them talk about change," one miner told the crowd. "We don't need change. We need to take what's working in America and keep it working."

Ron Paul spoke toward the end, arguing to repeal the Fed ("We'd all be better off," he said), cut all foreign aid, and end the country's role as policeman of the world. When he began his standard argument against having so many American military bases overseas and in favor of bringing American troops home from Korea and Japan, people toward the back of the crowd began to object. "God bless the military!" they hollered.

Paul moved on to the need to keep our military strong, and the hecklers began cheering again. Then the crowd sang "God Bless America," twice, following along with the words on two JumboTrons on the lawn. On the stage, the whole Tea Party amalgam gathered: the coal miners, Lord Monckton,

Ron Paul, Victoria Jackson with her ukulele, the national coordinators from Tea Party Patriots, Dick Armey, and the Freedom-Works staffers.

Matt Kibbe told the people on the lawn that they would see them again at the 9/12 rally in September. Until then, there was work to be done out in the states.

CHAPTER NINE

"I have a message, a message from the Tea Party"

Charles Merwin Grayson III was bred to be a United States Senator.

A fifth-generation Kentuckian and the son of a prominent banker in the northern part of the state, he had never known a time—or so it seemed—when a superlative was not attached to his name. Known to all as "Trey," he was valedictorian of his high school class, student council president, basketball star, a governor's scholar, elected to the statewide academic competition hall of fame. He went to Harvard, where he graduated with honors and was chosen for the board of the Institute of Politics, then came home and graduated at the top of his class at the University of Kentucky College of Law, a training ground for the state's political class. He had been the youngest secretary of state in the country, the only Kentuckian chosen for the Republican platform committee in 2008, one of only two Republicans to be reelected to a statewide office in a year when scandal had engulfed the party's governor and the national tide had turned blue. The Aspen Institute gave him a fellowship for promising young leaders, the Republican National Committee named him a "rising star." And so on.

Trey Grayson had been in high school when he met Mitch McConnell, the state's senior U.S. senator, at a private fundraiser. "He wants your job," Grayson's mother told McConnell. It was a joke, sort of. Grayson had won a student athletic award; when the school secretary was filling out the questionnaire that went with it, she asked him what he wanted to do.

"Politics," he said.

"What, like a senator?" she asked.

"Yeah, put down senator," he replied.

It was that kind of thing. It wasn't clear what office it would be, or even which party—Grayson was a Democrat until after college, because that's what his parents were—but his résumé had been made for politics. A sturdy six-foot-five, he even looked the part.

Starting as the head of Young Professionals for Bush in 2000, he had spent a decade working his way up the state's Republican establishment, a process he described as though it were effortless: "I knocked on the doors and licked the envelopes, and then decided at thirty-one to run for Secretary of State and made it."

In 2010, Kentucky's junior senator, an irascible baseball Hall of Famer named Jim Bunning, was facing a tough reelection fight. He had barely won a second term in 2004. So McConnell, now the Senate minority leader and so thick in Kentucky politics that the state Republican Party headquarters had been named after him, nudged Bunning into retirement. But not before securing Grayson, who had been pondering a run for governor, to run for the seat.

In almost any other year, that would have been the end of it. Trey Grayson would have won in a cakewalk, and at thirty-eight added "youngest senator" to his collection of superlatives. In almost any other year, his primary opponent, Rand Paul, would have suffered a similar fate as his father, Ron Paul, whose run for president in 2008 was powered by a core of supporters that was passionate but not big enough for victory.

But 2010 was not any other year. It was the year of the Tea Party.

No campaign better captured the trends that had converged in the Tea Party than the race for the Republican nomination for the U.S. Senate in Kentucky; no contest would be a better test of the new movement's electoral power. Yes, it had won with Scott Brown in Massachusetts, but that was about saying no to health care reform. It had won in Utah, but that was about getting rid of an incumbent who had dared to reach across the aisle. Charlie Crist had been driven from the primary in Florida, but Marco Rubio pointedly identified himself as a conservative, not a Tea Party candidate.

If Trey Grayson was Establishment, Rand Paul was Tea Party, having attended some of the earliest rallies in Kentucky. "If they had cards," he said, "I'd be a card-carrying member." And through his father, he laid claim to a long embrace of libertarian philosophy. (Though many people assumed he had been named for the libertarian novelist and philosopher Ayn Rand, the truth was that his full name was Randal.) He brought together the idealistic wing that had started the movement and the angry wing that had swelled its ranks; the young and tech-savvy Tea Partiers and the older ones concerned about taxes and the national debt. As an eye surgeon, with no previous political experience, he had an anti-Washington appeal that resonated with the people who had been cheering the

Tea Party from the sidelines and rooting to throw the bums out. In the videos on his campaign website outlining his policy positions, he appeared wearing scrubs, suggesting he had more important things to do.

Paul had the backing of Sarah Palin and Dick Armey. He also had his father's national fundraising network, so he would not lack for cash. (This one would be hard work *and* Daddy's money.)

Paul's supporters spoke about his campaign in terms of a mission, and so did he, declaring that a "reckoning" was at hand. It was a reckoning for big government, but also for the Republican Party. The Republican establishment knew it had a problem; they had known it from the uproar over Charlie Crist in Florida, and when Dede Scozzafava was driven from the race in upstate New York. Those contests might have suggested that the only adjustment needed was to follow the script from the past: move further to the right, especially on social issues. After all, the challengers, Marco Rubio and Doug Hoffman, were more reliably prolife and anti–gay marriage. But Paul's campaign made clear to Republicans in Washington that this wasn't just a center-versus-right debate. This was antigovernment; this was anti-Them. As much as Trey Grayson was going to have to contend with Rand Paul, the Republicans were going to have to contend with the Tea Party. They had hoped they could harness its energy toward victory in the midterm elections. Rand Paul made clear that the Tea Party might actually make things more difficult.

The Tea Party was going to be tested, too, on the strength of its unlikely coalition. The libertarians who saw Paul as their standard-bearer recognized that the Tea Party had been a boon for their numbers and that he was their best chance for a big electoral victory. But they worried that the new grassroots recruits did not truly understand the implications of small government, that popular programs like Social Security were inconsistent with constitutional fidelity, as they saw it.

"There's a larger group that doesn't get it," said Tim Quinn, an environmental consultant in Louisville who had campaigned for Ron Paul in 2008 before jumping on the son's bandwagon. "People want change," he said, "but they need to look deeper."

The Tea Party had always been better about defining what it was against than what it was for. As Rand Paul toured Kentucky, he talked about what he supported, his interpretations of Austrian economics, and the Constitution. Voters talked about a range of grievances and, mostly, economic anxiety. It wasn't always clear that they were really listening to what he was saying. Until the end.

The Republicans who recruited Trey Grayson to run for Jim Bunning's seat did not see Rand Paul coming. But plenty of others did. They came to Rand Paul through Ron Paul. And they described coming to Ron Paul as if it were a religious conversion.

Tim Quinn and his wife Sheri, a civil engineer, marked it to her pregnancy with their first child. She wanted a natural childbirth, without pain medication, but the doctors kept talking about various interventions and regulations about having a midwife attend the delivery. "We learned that we're not free," Sheri said. "We were just regular dinks"—double income, no kids—"who went to college and wanted to make a health decision. Now you're pigeonholed as wacky. I made a birth plan and they laughed at it." Later, when their children approached school age, they decided to homeschool them, and discovered another raft of regulation. "Until people run up against something they want to do but can't do it, they're going to be apathetic," she said. Around that time they "met" Ron Paul—"in his online presence," as Sheri explained.

The Quinns liked the clarity of the Constitution and Ron Paul's fidelity to it. They liked the Austrian economic theories with their emphasis on protecting the rights of even the smallest minority of one and their principle that the government should never be able to do what individuals can do for themselves. Ron Paul argued that establishing a military was one thing, but just as you can't delegate a neighbor to steal a car you covet, you can't legitimately delegate the government to take taxes from one person to use for another person's benefit. The Quinns thought that Ron Paul had integrity, that he was willing to speak his mind. "He had a consistent message," Sheri said. "That's what really resonated with me." They researched the things he talked about and decided they were true.

"It was all she wrote after that," Sheri said. She became the Jefferson County coordinator for the 2008 Ron Paul campaign, and got to know Rand Paul as he appeared as a surrogate for his father on the campaign trail. When Ron Paul quit the presidential race and reshaped his organization as the Campaign for Liberty, she became the Kentucky state coordinator, organizing Constitution courses and online groups to read Bastiat's *The Law*.

Ron Paul had been scaring many conservatives for years with his anti-interventionist beliefs. On national security, he had long argued that the Founding Fathers did not envision the United States being the policeman of the world, a position that did not find much support on the right when the nation was engaged in two wars. And at home, Ron Paul's doctrinaire libertarianism had led him into relationships with politically unsavory groups. In 2008 he had been the keynote speaker at the fiftieth anniversary dinner of the John Birch Society, which William F. Buckley Jr. had exiled from the conservative movement in the 1960s for its racist advocacy. At the dinner, held in Joe McCarthy's hometown of Appleton, Wisconsin, Ron Paul called the Birchers "a great patriotic organization featuring an educational program solidly based on Constitutional principles."

But what Ron Paul's fans focused on were his economic theories, which to them merely advocated a solid defense against government intrusion in the lives of individuals.

Ryan Renshaw, a burly thirty-eight-year-old car dealer from Bowling Green, described his discovery of Ron Paul as a late night "epiphany" in front of his computer after his kids went to bed. He considered himself a conservative Republican—"hawkish," he said. In 2007, a friend sent him an email with three attachments: a speech Ron Paul had given about the Federal Reserve in the 1970s, another given by Ronald Reagan about the size of the federal government, and *America: Freedom to Fascism*, a film by Aaron Russo (the producer of such films as *Trading Places*, *The Rose*, and *Wise Guys*) that criticized the Federal Reserve, the Internal Revenue Service, and the Sixteenth Amendment, which had authorized a federal income tax. Renshaw started reading about the creation of the Fed in 1913, and he was won over by Ron Paul's argument that by printing more money, the Fed was imposing a "hidden tax" by devaluing the dollars already in circulation.

"I couldn't find anything to dispute it," he said. "My paradigm of the whole United States just changed on a dime. I went from being a loyal Republican, voting the whole Republican line, to really watching what these guys are saying." Something he read online directed him to *The Real George Washington*, one of a series of books published by Cleon Skousen's National Center for Constitutional Studies—the same Cleon Skousen who wrote *The 5000 Year Leap*—that aims to discover the Founding Fathers' real views by looking at their letters and other writings. Renshaw came to believe that the Founders did not intend the Constitution as a document that would be subject to interpretation over time, and that Congress had increasingly abused or disregarded it since the New Deal. "America's financial health was more at risk of destroying the nation than any outside threat," he concluded. "I became a Ron Paul person, even though we probably disagree on national security."

Ron Paul supporters had already invoked the memory of the Boston Tea Party in December 2007, organizing a "moneybomb" for his campaign on the anniversary of the original 1773 uprising. The idea was to solicit small donations that would accumulate and explode into one big donation that day. It worked: the campaign took in nearly $6 million. But in the actual race for delegates in 2008, Paul's campaign never took off, and he returned to Capitol Hill, where he remained a quirky presence in Congress, voting against appropriations that he believed were not authorized by the Constitution: Medicare and Medicaid, relief for Hurricane Katrina victims, a congressional gold medal for Ronald Reagan.

The economic collapse in the fall of 2008 created a more fertile environment for his small-government ideas. But the crisis "wasn't early enough for the 2008 election," Sheri Quinn said, with regret.

Rand Paul, Ron's third son, had caught the bug for politicking after filling in for his father on the campaign trail. Other than starting a group called Kentucky Taxpayers United in 1994, he had little political experience. But at forty-six, he was attractive, a more silver tongued version of his father, with a wife, Kelley, who looked as if she would fit in perfectly at a Senate wives' tea, and three handsome sons.

When the word began getting out that Jim Bunning might not run again, Rand Paul called Chris Derry, the former owner of an asset management business who had founded the Bluegrass Institute to promote free-market ideas around the state. Derry suggested that he talk to David Adams, who wrote a blog on state politics for the institute.

On February 26, 2009, the day before the first wave of Tea Parties across the country, Adams posted the news that Rand Paul was thinking of running for the Senate. Suddenly, the hits to his obscure Kentucky politics blog spiked. "It was the blog post that went round the world," Adams said. On websites for Ron Paul acolytes, like the DailyPaul and Paul Forums, readers cheered. "First Senate, then Paul/Paul 2012!" exulted one commenter.

In a speech in Lexington in mid-March, Rand Paul criticized the Republican establishment for abandoning small-government principles, but he also warned his fellow libertarians that they had to change their approach. If the Republicans didn't want the libertarians, "they will shrink," he said. "They are losing ground. They need us. So we need to convince them of that. But some of it is us, too. We have to convince them in a nice and friendly way. They were afraid we were going to take over. We weren't; we didn't have the numbers to do that. We still need to go, we need to be nice to these people, and shake their hands. But we do need to transcend what we were. We need to be bigger."

The Tea Party movement was the way to get bigger. And David Adams was already working to build it in Kentucky. On

Facebook, he had heard about a viewing party for Glenn Beck's 9/12 special at GattiTown Pizza in Lexington, and when he showed up, he discovered more than a hundred people there, many of whom had driven in from around the state. A week later, on March 21, he was the emcee for the state's first Tea Party rally, in Lexington. Seeing the crowds there, he began planning more Tea Parties.

Adams began inviting Rand Paul to speak at the events. And in June, he pitched himself to the prospective candidate as a campaign manager. "At some point we were going to have to turn this into something bigger than hundreds of people venting," Adams said. "As we got started with the campaign, the Tea Party theme was a pretty easy one to plug into. That's where the energy was."

Paul called it the "perfect storm." "It's the perfect constellation of a lot of factors coming together all at once," he said. And it was. Sheri Quinn's Campaign for Liberty was working with Tea Party groups on rallies, the Tea Party groups were working with the 9/12ers. People were mad about government bailouts, the lagging economy, and then the health care debate. Paul was eager to be the leader of the new force. "I want to be out there telling people what I think it is," he said. "Because it is what we create it to be."

In August, when Paul was ready to officially declare his candidacy, he did it from a Tea Party–approved stage: *The Glenn Beck Show*.

Trey Grayson, with his pedigree, his name recognition, and his Republican connections, started out fifteen points ahead in the polls. But Paul tapped into the public mood. "A Tea Party tidal wave is coming!" he liked to tell his crowds. Outside a courthouse in Independence, he told a group of about a hundred people gathered in a light rain that one of his first acts as a U.S. senator would be to band together with five or six other conservatives and refuse to let Congress do any work if it could not agree to amend the Constitution to require a balanced budget.

"Let's just stop it for a week," Paul said. "Let's just stop it up and let's invite the Tea Party up and let's fill the Mall and let's debate a balanced budget amendment and let them explain why they can't do it."

"Gridlock!" cheered a retired Marine with a long gray ponytail. The crowd echoed approvingly.

Paul's campaign staff, a combination of former Ron Paulites and local Tea Party leaders, relentlessly mocked Grayson as a country club Republican, referring to him by his full name, including the Roman numeral, instead of "Trey." Paul, by contrast, came off as authentic.

In early April 2010, six weeks before the Republican primary, Paul was touring the state in a luxury bus owned by Ryan Renshaw's sister, who had dropped out of theater school in New York City and become a NASCAR driver. David Adams was rallying the crowd of about a hundred people gathered for a Tea Party in the parking lot outside Ol' Harvey's Eats when the bus pulled in. Paul ambled toward the front of the crowd, wearing a short-sleeved denim shirt and brown rubber-soled shoes, his hair tousled. As he listened to the warm-up speakers, his head down, brow furrowed, he gave the sense of a man with a lot on his mind. It was an appealing pose to Tea Partiers who believed that the founders intended us to have citizen legislators rather than governing elites, men who served their country and then went back to what they really wanted to do, which was to tend their farms. As Adams introduced him, Paul demurred: "I thought we were going to have some music first." His three young sons took the makeshift stage with guitars, singing "This Land is Your Land," and "America the Beautiful." Then the crowd joined in to sing "Happy Birthday" to Robert, the youngest.

Paul stayed long at every stop to answer questions, and he gave expansive, sometimes rambling answers. His message was more apocalyptic than the usual uplift of a politician's speech. "The end is coming, the times are growing short to fix the situation." he said ominously. He often quoted Thomas Paine—"These are the times that try men's souls"—or the Canadian band Rush, known for their libertarian views: "Glittering prizes and endless compromises / shatter the illusion of integrity." The glittering prizes, Paul told the audience outside Ol' Harvey's, were the pork-barrel projects that politicians bring home even though there is no money to pay for them. It was like the last days of Rome, he told the audience, where leaders used bread and circuses to placate the mob.

"When they promise you things, they're promising something they don't have to give," he said. "They have picked the pig clean."

But if his speeches were downers, his crowds loved them. To them, the language felt honest.

"It's really freeing to see people coming out for the Tea Party who would never have said anything," said Cliff Pike, an Episcopalian minister who had retired to Kentucky after his last parish in West Chester, Pennsylvania. Wearing a pressed gingham dress shirt and khakis, he was leaving the rally in Lawrenceburg with a RAND PAUL U.S. SENATE 2010 lawn sign. "They don't usually talk politics or religion. As a minister, I couldn't even put up a sign on my lawn."

"It's hard for us to come out here and, you know, clap clap," agreed his wife, Nancy. "We don't usually show our emotions that way."

The Pikes had been to their first Tea Party in Louisville a year earlier, concerned about the bailouts of the banks and auto companies, the proposed cap-and-trade legislation, and the prospect of health care reform. "All of a sudden you've had it up to here and you want to do something," Cliff Pike said. "It's like the frog in the kettle—only I'm a human being and we're smart enough to know we're in hot water as a country."

They were also angry about how Tea Party supporters had been portrayed in the media. "These were stockbrokers, university professors, normal people," Cliff said. "You don't see racists or bigots. You see your next door neighbors."

Rand Paul told it like it was, Cliff said. "Grayson's a career politician. It's about time we broke the mold."

While Rand Paul brought a message of strict constitutional interpretation and smaller government, his audiences, like the Tea Party itself, greeted him with sprawling concerns. They wanted him to be the answer to all of them.

Mostly they asked about jobs, and how to bring them back. A woman at Bruce's Country Store in Mason complained that food safety laws were hurting small farmers; Paul agreed, criticizing laws that banned the sale of raw milk and then those that regulated homeschooling. At the rally in Lawrenceburg, a woman asked his position on cyberbullying. Paul said that he thought schools had rules on that, and that parents had to take some responsibility for knowing what their children were writing and seeing online. "You have to balance freedom of expression," he said.

"They're taking advantage of freedom of speech to use slander and violence," the woman insisted.

Paul urged her, again, to work with school officials. The woman persisted. Kelley Paul, standing in the audience, smiled hard and said in a sweet Kentucky singsong, "I think he's answered the question."

~

While Rand Paul barely had to arrange campaign events—the Tea Party was doing it for him—Trey Grayson took a more traditional route. As Paul was crisscrossing Kentucky on his bus, Grayson was finishing a tour of the medical center in Pikeville, in the eastern part of the state, and heading to a local Rotary Club luncheon. "You're still on the fourth floor at the Landmark?" he said to a hospital publicist and Rotary Club member, an old friend from their days in statewide high school academic competitions.

The Rotarians welcomed him as a familiar face. "He knows us, he knows where we are," the president said, introducing him. Grayson, in a black suit and a white shirt with mono-grammed cuffs, spoke briefly and then threw the floor open to questions. "Or we can talk about basketball," he quipped. The publisher of the local paper wanted to know Grayson's thoughts on the unfolding coal mining disaster just over the border in West Virginia. Grayson offered little in the way of emotion, but said he was angry about an earlier guidance issued by the Environmental Protection Agency. In the Sen-ate, he said, he wanted to serve on the Energy Committee. "I've talked to McConnell about this," he added.

In Inez, where Lyndon Johnson had once stood on Tom Fletcher's porch to declare his war on poverty, Grayson worked a courthouse empty except for a couple of employees and a judge. ("You running against a crazy man, you know that?" the judge, Kelly Callaham, said.) Then he went to a bank across the street where Mike Duncan, the former chair-man of the Republican National Committee and one of the people responsible for getting Grayson into Republican politics, was chief executive. Then it was on to a late afternoon meeting with a local doctor. The strategy, Grayson's aides said, was to meet with influential leaders who would spread the word among voters.

The polls had been leaning Rand Paul's way for months, but Grayson still seemed surprised to find the race so stacked against him. "The Republican primary in which I find myself" was how he described his race to the Rotarians.

Grayson's time in public service had been all about making government better: he had worked on election reform initiatives statewide and nationally, tried to ease bureaucratic hassles in the secretary of state's office by putting more documents online, established a commission to find better ways to finance higher education, and started a program to teach students to be more informed voters. He bristled that Rand Paul had tagged him as the "establishment" candidate. As if being an incumbent was a bad thing?

"I'm not going to deny that as an incumbent I have a relationship with a lot of party regulars, but this is a race about who's going to be best in Washington," he said. "I don't think that label's an accurate assessment of who I am and what I've done or what my record is. I ran for the first time just a few years ago. Here's a guy who's the son—I mean, it's kind of funny when he throws that at me—here's the guy whose dad's been in Congress twenty-something years, and has inherited a national organization.

"He's very articulate, but I mean, how many smart people are there in the state who have the intelligence to run for Senate but don't have the name recognition or the network or something like that? You know, if he were Rand Smith, ophthalmologist from Bowling Green, Kentucky, we wouldn't be talking about him. I just kind of find it ironic, here I am, I've just worked my way up through campaigns, I'm the first person in my family to run for office, I got reelected in a really tough environment, I've stood up to McConnell, I've stood up to our former governor, I've stood up to leaders of my party, I've stood up to Democrats. I'm the one who's cleaned up and has this record. I'm not the country club Republican who lives in a gated community whose dad's in Congress."

Grayson said he understood the frustration among voters. But it was like being stuck in a traffic jam. "You can honk on the horn and it makes you feel good, but you're still stuck in traffic behind that car," he said. "You're better off getting around, passing, and keep going. And I think in this campaign, Paul is the guy who is attractive to the people who are honking on their horn. Because I don't think he is going to be able to navigate Washington and actually get stuff done."

In the desire for radical change, Grayson said, people had lost any appreciation for the measured but effective solution. "He says he will not vote for any budget bill that is not balanced," he said, talking about Paul. "What if we had a compromise that lowered the budget to zero over ten years? That would imply that over nine of those ten years you would vote for an unbalanced budget, but he would always say no to that." Most Republicans, and most Kentuckians, Grayson argued, would support the compromise, "because it's a more productive way of dealing with the problem."

Grayson tried everything to recapture the lead. He ran ads that portrayed Paul's ideas as "strange"—or "Too Kooky for Kentucky," as the name of a blog put up by a Grayson supporter called them. He ran an Internet ad comparing a clip of Rand Paul explaining his father's view that American foreign policy had encouraged the 9/11 attacks with one of Jeremiah Wright, President Obama's controversial former pastor, declaring that America's chickens had come home to roost. He pointed out that Rand Paul had called coal "a very dirty form of energy" (in a state with 17,000 coal workers) and argued that he would not support the wars in Iraq and Afghanistan (in a state with two major army bases).

Nothing seemed to stick.

In Washington, foreign policy conservatives circulated an email warning that Rand Paul shared his father's views against military intervention and against the Patriot Act, and that he would be a weak link in the war on terror. Former Vice President Dick Cheney endorsed Grayson, saying that the country needed U.S. senators who "will work to strengthen our commitment to a strong national defense and to whom this is not just a political game."

Pointing out that a candidate did not support the Patriot Act might have worked against a Democrat in 2004. But 2010 wasn't about the old fights. It was about the establishment. Toward the end, the race became a proxy for McConnell versus Bunning—Washington ways versus those who had been shoved aside by them. Paul defended Bunning when he came under criticism for holding up a bill that would have extended unemployment benefits, on the grounds that it would add to the deficit. Bunning in turn endorsed Paul, saying that he would stand up to Washington's profligate spending. McConnell, who had hoped to stay neutral, then endorsed Grayson.

But McConnell had already invited Kentucky Republicans to participate in a "unity rally" on Saturday, May 22, four days after the primary, no matter who won. That was when Paul's campaign staffers knew they had the race in the bag.

~

The conservatives on Twitter began jumping as polls closed in Kentucky on Tuesday, May 18, just as they had after Rick Santelli's rant fifteen months earlier. "Randslide!" someone declared it, and others picked up the phrase; #randslide soon became its own hashtag, to identify tweets about Paul's victory.

Rand Paul had won by twenty-four percentage points.

More than a hundred supporters had gathered for the victory party at the Bowling Green Country Club, with its lush greens, popping azaleas, and limpid turquoise pool. Around the fireplace on the outdoor patio, they clinked beer bottles and tumblers of scotch. Andrew Demers, the campaign's twenty-eight-year-old political director and a veteran of the Ron Paul New Hampshire campaign, had invited Rand's father to join the celebration, and Ron stood by proudly as his son stuffed a pipe. Jim Johnson, a seventy-year-old car dealer and a neighbor of Rand Paul's, said he still thought of himself as a conservative, but he was getting to be more of a libertarian. "I'm not 100 percent libertarian, I'm about 78 percent," he said, "but I'm getting there."

Sarah Palin called Paul as soon as the results were in, followed by Mitt Romney. Finally, Paul came out to the booming sounds of the Rush lyric and the cheers of the crowd. He paid tribute to his wife, his sons, his siblings, his parents, his staff, and mostly, the movement that had propelled him.

"I have a message, a message from the Tea Party," he proclaimed. "We have come to take our government back. . . . We are encountering a day of reckoning and this movement,

this Tea Party movement is a message to Washington that
we're unhappy and that we want things done differently. The
Tea Party movement is huge. The mandate of our victory
tonight is huge. What you have done and what we are doing
can transform America."

As Rand Paul departed the stage, supporters and reporters
mobbed Ron Paul. Supporters asked for autographs, and congratulated him as the one truly responsible for the victory that
night. "What you did for Rand is what Barry Goldwater did
for Ronald Reagan," one gushed.

The success of his son's campaign, the elder Paul told
reporters, showed that Americans were finally catching on to
Austrian economics. He had noticed it in 2007, that college
students started nodding their heads when he mentioned von
Mises and Hayek—ideas he had been talking about for forty
years. Now, he said, the word was spreading, and politicians
would have to pay attention. "And get rid of the power people,"
he said, "the people who run the show, the people who think
they're above everybody else. That's what the people are sick
and tired of, that's the message."

The primary had been open to Republicans only, which
meant that it reflected the state's most conservative voters. To
win in November, Rand Paul would have to win among Democrats, who dominated Kentucky voter rolls. He vowed to resist
calls to moderate his message, to abandon the Tea Party.

But his honeymoon, as he called it, did not last long. By
the next day it was apparent that the Tea Party might not
maintain its appeal under the new national spotlight.

Appearing on *The Rachel Maddow Show* on MSNBC,
Rand Paul said he disagreed with the provisions of the 1964
Civil Rights Act that required businesses and restaurants to
serve blacks. He said that while he abhorred discrimination,

he did not like the idea of telling private business owners what to do. (When pushed, he said he would have voted to approve the statute if he had been in the Senate at the time.) Earlier in the day, he had questioned the legality of the Americans with Disabilities Act on similar grounds. But it was his dismissal of the landmark civil rights legislation that drew the most heat.

Republicans came down hard. Senator Jon Kyl of Arizona, the minority whip and thus a top lieutenant to Mitch McConnell, said, "I hope he can separate the theoretical and the interesting and the hypothetical questions that college students debate until two A.M. from the actual votes we have to cast based on real legislation here." Senator Lindsey Graham of South Carolina went on record, as he put it, standing up for how the courts and Congress had expanded the definition of the commerce clause to include civil rights. "That's not a heavy lift for me," he said. McConnell suggested that Paul give up national interviews for a while.

Paul canceled his appearance on *Meet the Press* for that Sunday, which to some Washington insiders was only marginally less shocking than casting doubt on the Civil Rights Act. But his campaign continued to see the fracas as an old political game.

When Paul emerged a few days later, appearing in his scrubs to speak at a Lions Club luncheon in Bowling Green, he blamed his Democratic opponent, Jack Conway, for first telling reporters that he opposed the act. "That's the bad thing about politics," he said. "Not only do you have to run to defend your position, you've got to defend the position they make up for you, and that makes it hard."

To David Adams, the remark had been improperly characterized as a "gaffe."

"In truth," he said, "he's talking in great detail in an attempt to answer a question. That's the risk you run being Rand Paul and being the type of person who will stand there on the record and on video and answer any question. That's a great opportunity for political gamesmanship, but it also sends a message to the electorate that is tired of being soundbited, an electorate that wants a politician who will stand there and on his own tackle the questions, whether the truth is difficult or not."

"It's more than just a political gaffe," he said, "It's what this movement is about."

It was true. In focusing on the civil rights question, the media had gotten only part of the story. The truth was broader, and it would be difficult.

Rand Paul didn't just quibble with the Civil Rights Act. He didn't just want to get rid of the Department of Education and the Department of Energy—goals dear to conservatives for decades. In his vision, and in the vision of the Tea Party purists, the New Deal and much of what came afterward was unconstitutional, as was much of what Americans had come to expect government to do for the past century.

Paul said he would not vote for any legislation that was not authorized by the Constitution, and he liked to tell crowds that Congress could balance the budget if it just got rid of all the unauthorized things. These lines got big applause. And he was correct that the only way to take more than a nibble out of the national debt was to cut programs like Social Security and Medicare.

But to the many people who had come to the Tea Party movement frustrated about the economy and the health care legislation, liberty and freedom were warm patriotic ideas. Fiscal responsibility meant not bailing out the car companies or the people who had taken out mortgages they couldn't afford. It meant cutting waste and earmarks. They might like the notion of getting rid of the progressive income tax or even the Fed. But it wasn't clear that they understood that the strict constitutionalist approach would eliminate benefits to the elderly, subsidies for students who could not afford college on their own, laws that made sure banks couldn't disappear with people's savings overnight.

"I think he's unrealistic," said Donna Wolbe, who voted for Trey Grayson at the same polling place where Rand Paul voted in Bowling Green. "He doesn't say anything that I don't agree with," especially on taxes and health care. "It's just that it's so far from where we are. You can't do away with things all of a sudden. We have to think about what's best for people."

This is America, as Rick Santelli had said. What he left out was that in America, though people loved to hate big government, they also liked their government programs when they were helping, which in many cases, they were. People might get frustrated with Congress or the federal bureaucracy. But they did not want to leave old people relying on the whims of the market or charity for health and security in their sunset years. The Depression had pretty much answered that question, and nobody since then had been able to meaningfully cut the size of government. Even Ronald Reagan wasn't much interested in it.

The Tea Party was out to try again. And as the movement's most visible success story, Rand Paul's campaign was either going to be its Run for the Roses—or the moment the bloom fell off.

Epilogue

On May 18, as the Republican establishment was turning on a dime to congratulate Rand Paul on his win in Kentucky, the Republican Party in Pennsylvania was threatening to have Jennifer Stefano arrested.

As primary day dawned, pouring rain, Stefano and her Tea Party candidates for the Republican committee positions went to the polls, where they planned to stand outside the no-politicking zone and hand out sample ballots asking people to vote for them.

When they arrived, the ten Tea Party candidates for the state committee found constables there to seize the sample ballots and instruct them to leave. "They're going to pull me out of here in shackles seven months pregnant!" Stefano reported from her polling place. "I feel like Abbie Hoffman!"

For all that the Tea Party movement had borrowed from the left, the notion of this blonde suburban wife as the long-haired sixties radical was comical. Stefano, however, was not laughing.

The night before, in her final email, she had prepared her troops for the possibility of resistance from the party establishment. She had heard from Republicans sympathetic to the Tea Party that party officials had been spreading the word that the Tea Party candidates were "illegitimate" and should be defeated. "Our party, so entrenched in their petty politics and turf wars, has turned on its own people to protect their own interests," she warned her recruits.

> That means ALL OF YOU must be STRONG!!!!!!!!!!!!!!! LET ME MODIFY MY USUAL ASSERTION: WE HAVE BETTER IDEAS AND BETTER MANNERS . . . SO BE POLITE . . . BUT NEVER BE AFRAID TO BE TOUGH. . . .
> THEY WILL SEEK TO INTIMIDATE, SMEAR AND DEFAME YOU. THEY WILL SEEK TO TAKE ADVANTAGE OF THIS BEING THE FIRST POLITICAL RACE FOR MOST OF YOU . . . AND THEY WILL TRY TO EXPLOIT YOUR INEXPERIENCE!!!!!! I AM TELLING YOU NOW: GIRD YOUR LOINS.

She signed off the way she had at her training sessions: "Get up early and . . . WIN!"

But Stefano had expected a fair fight, one decided at the ballot box. Instead, the party-endorsed candidates had gone to court that morning to get an injunction against the Tea Party candidates, arguing that the sample ballots did not indicate who had authorized or paid for them, as Pennsylvania election law required. No one had told the Tea Party candidates about the hearing. By the time their lawyers could offer a counterargument—that the law applied only to candidates for public office, not party offices, and that the ballots indicated the name of the printing company that donated them—many of the people Stefano had recruited to run for the positions had gone home. Officials had told them they could not be at the polling station even to shake voters' hands.

"I mean, I expected to get thugged up and intimidated at the polls by the Democrats, but by Republicans?" Stefano said later. "Unconscionable. I think the GOP is happy to pat us on the head and say 'What good little protesters you are! Go out and cause problems for the Democrats.' But when we finally want to have a say about the direction of the party, the GOP did not and does not want us involved."

Pat Poprik, the chairwoman of the Bucks County Republican Party, said she found it unseemly for the Tea Partiers to try to buck the endorsed candidates. "This is a party office. This is not a public office. This is our election," she told the local paper. "It is highly unusual for people who have never done a thing for the party to run for state committee."

Stefano had made the best of it. After the constables seized her ballots, she held up a copy of the injunction and declared to the voters within earshot, "The Republican establishment just sued me for daring to have a voice in the party they control. My name is Jennifer Stefano, and I respectfully ask for your vote." In the election for the state party position, she won the four districts in her town, but not countywide. Still, she won a local committee seat. And of her one hundred recruits for the local committee positions, nearly seventy won.

The Republican Party, she argued, had been the real loser. "More people now realize there is a war on two fronts," she said. "In D.C. with the Obama administration and at home against the Republican treachery that allowed people like Obama and the other progressives to flourish."

She was taking the long view: "The people who have failed to represent us in the Republican Party have got to be targeted, they have got to go, if it takes four, six, eight, ten years. I think most machines look at people like us and think, 'They will go away. These dumb housewives are going to go back and have babies and we'll outlast these bastards.' It's not happening this time."

~

As the Tea Party headed toward the 2010 midterm elections, it continued to defy assumptions, all the neat categories people tried to place around it. It was not just a group of especially conservative Republicans. It remained, at its heart, more anti-establishment than anything else. It had stirred energy among Republican voters, but that energy might just hurt the Republican Party.

In the Republican primaries that spring, being the candidate identified with the Tea Party was not always the electoral charm that many would have predicted in January, when the movement helped Scott Brown score his upset. In June, the Tea Party candidate in the Republican primary for the U.S. Senate seat in California, a state assemblyman named Chuck DeVore, lost to Carly Fiorina, the former Hewlett-Packard chief executive, who was supported by establishment figures like John McCain. But in Nevada, the Tea Party had coalesced around Sharron Angle, and she beat Danny Tarkanian and Sue Lowden, the onetime frontrunners.

After Rand Paul's humbling experience in the national media after his primary win, it should have surprised no one that Angle immediately faced tough questions about statements she had made about wanting to phase out Medicare and Social Security. She was criticized for her support of Oath Keepers, the group that had set up under the Tea Party umbrella and was stirring rumors that the federal government was going to force Americans into concentration camps. The National Republican Senatorial Committee took Angle off the interview circuit for a few weeks so it could "staff her up," as officials said. Her campaign soon featured a new website, with a less expansive explanation of her policy positions. "We must keep the promise of Social Security," it declared. Gone was her mention of abolishing the tax code. (Reid's campaign soon found a way to keep her old website alive, resurrecting it under a new site that it called "The Real Sharron Angle.")

Rand Paul also shook up his campaign staff, bringing in a veteran from his father's presidential campaign to replace David Adams, who had made him a Tea Party sensation. As Mitch McConnell had suggested, Paul began declining national interviews, and he now asked Kentucky reporters to submit their questions in writing.

The Republican Party establishment worried that both candidates might alienate independents and conservative Democrats with their Tea Party ideas, costing the party two elections that should otherwise be easy for it to win. But Paul and Angle still had an advantage in the general election: the public's anger at the Democrats and at the federal government. Paul's Democratic opponent, Jack Conway, was the state attorney general, and he had declined to join other state attorneys general in suing the federal government over the health care law, which was unpopular in Kentucky. In Nevada, Harry Reid may have had a great campaign organization, but few politicians were more associated with Washington in the minds of voters.

But for all the antigovernment feeling in the air, the reaction to the massive oil spill on a BP rig in the Gulf of Mexico that began on April 20—the largest in the nation's history—suggested that the public was far from resolving its love-hate relationship with big government. After BP agreed to President Obama's demand that it set up a $20 billion fund to pay claims from the spill, Representative Joe Barton, a Texas Republican, apologized to the company's chief executive, accusing the White House of having engaged in "extortion." The Republican Party's leaders forced Barton to retract his words, but conservatives defended him. His outburst reflected the free-market worldview that businesses should be left alone to conduct their affairs. Rand Paul, before he was silenced, had also criticized the administration's tough treatment of BP as "unAmerican." At the same time, the oil slick had reminded many people of the benefits of a strong central government. Faced with pictures of wildlife and marshes slicked with oil, and the prospect of damaged beaches and a devastated tourism industry, Americans told pollsters that they wanted the federal government to take a stronger hand in regulation. They trusted it more than BP to clean up the spill. It was the old dilemma: viscerally hating how reliant we are on government, but recognizing that reliance all the same.

～

The Tea Party groups were working to keep the movement's energy alive. They spent the summer planning for big events coming up—Glenn Beck's rally in Washington in late August, the FreedomWorks 9/12 march in the capital in September, the National Tea Party Unity Convention planned for Las Vegas in mid-October. FreedomWorks was offering a special deal for Glenn Beck fans: become a FreedomWorks member and get a special Tea Party action kit as well as a "Don't Tread on Me" flag. Dick Armey and Matt Kibbe underscored the groups' central role in the movement by publishing a book, *Give Us Liberty: A Tea Party Manifesto*, which included a manual for starting a Tea Party protest, right down to what to say on the signs. The University of Chicago Press, meanwhile, reported that Beck had made Friedrich Hayek's *The Road to Serfdom* a bestseller after discussing the book on his show in June.

The movement was much more structured than it had been for the first 9/12 march on Washington the year before. Tea Party groups—local ones as well as the big ones like FreedomWorks—were more focused on organizing and spreading the word. Brendan Steinhauser was traveling across the country doing get-out-the-vote training. Tom Grimes, the "bus czar" from Indiana, had organized trips for both of the Washington rallies, but he was also planning to take a new educational program about the Constitution into schools in November. Run by a motivational speaker out of Texas, the program taught that Congress had to strictly adhere to its enumerated powers, and that it had abused its powers of taxing and spending.

But divisiveness and ugliness were still pushing into the movement at its fringes. In June, Joseph Farah, the World-NetDaily editor who had been pushing the Obama-is-not-a-citizen meme and was scheduled to speak again at the Tea Party convention in October, declared that the movement was "doomed to failure" if it ignored social issues for purely economic concerns. "We need to recognize sin when we see it," he wrote in his column. "We need to live by God's rules." William Gheen, the head of the conservative group Americans for Legal Immigration PAC, suggested to a Tea Party rally in Greenville, South Carolina, that Senator Lindsey Graham was supporting an immigration plan that provided legal status to guest workers because he feared that Democrats might otherwise expose him as gay. "I think, Senator Graham, you need to come forward and tell people about your alternative lifestyle and your homosexuality," he said, to which someone in the crowd replied, "Woo-hoo, that's right!" (Graham laughed this off in an interview with the *New York Times Magazine*: "I know it's really gonna upset a lot of gay men—I'm sure hundreds of 'em are gonna be jumping off the Golden Gate Bridge—but I ain't available. I ain't gay. Sorry.")

Many groups were trying to attach themselves to the Tea Party wagon, especially as the fight over immigration heated up with the passage in April of a new law in Arizona that gave state and local police broad powers to detain anyone they suspected of being in the country illegally. It was a reminder that the Tea Party movement remained divided over what its goals were supposed to be. The group Tea Party Nation urged its members to support the state of Arizona and sent out email alerts with the unsubstantiated assertion that President Obama was going to use an executive order to grant amnesty to every illegal immigrant in the country. Tea Party Patriots, which had become the largest Tea Party group, with 2,200 local affiliates, insisted that it would not get involved in the immigration debate, or in debates on any other social issues.

But when various anti-immigration groups called Diana Reimer and asked for her help, she could not say no. She was still busy with her Tea Party work—she had created seven groups in and around Philadelphia—but now she began working on her own with a coalition of groups that included some longtime conservative players, such as NumbersUSA and the Federation for American Immigration Reform. She and Don went to Tempe, Arizona, in late May to join in a rally in support of the Arizona law. "It's not to reinvent the wheel, it's just to get the word out for them more," she said. "You're either for amnesty or you're against it. My grandparents and great-grandparents came over here the right way, they learned how to speak English. They didn't take anybody's job."

As much as the lines were blurring between the Tea Party and more traditional conservative groups, the Tea Party itself was becoming more professionalized. Diana and four other national coordinators for Tea Party Patriots became full-time paid employees in the spring. Keli Carender had also become an employee at Tea Party Patriots, after the higher-ups at the nonprofit organization where she taught math complained that her political activities had created a conflict of interest. "I was like, wait a minute, our mission is to help people get out of their bad situation," she said. "How is that a conflict of interest with what I do? My goal is to get people off welfare and into jobs, as well."

Her superiors said they understood, but they were also concerned about safety. What if someone who disagreed with her came to one of her classes and hurt a student? Carender reminded them that she had always been careful not to iden-tify where she worked. But at a rally a few days later, she found herself getting nervous talking to reporters, worried about what her bosses would think. So she resigned. "I shouldn't be afraid of doing an interview," she said later. In addition to her work with Tea Party Patriots, she was working for a group called Sunshine Review on a project called StateBudgetSolutions .org, which took a free-market approach. She liked the work, she said; it felt like a positive contribution. It was the kind of "solution revolution" she had proposed in her first blog post as Liberty Belle in the winter of 2009.

Across the country, the Tea Party had certainly shaped the

political debate. It had encouraged fears among the public about health care reform, which meant that the Democrats would have to work harder to explain the new legislation's benefits to voters, particularly as the law would not take effect in full for several years. And the anger about health care had made energy reform a third-rail issue for Republicans and conservative Democrats who had once supported it.

The movement had shaped the Republican Party, too, stripping social issues of the prominence they had enjoyed for decades. On the campaign trail before the 2010 midterm elections, Republicans were declaring their intention to stop "out-of-control Washington spending" and reverse the health care legislation; they were talking little if at all about abortion and gay marriage, even after a federal judge in Massachusetts ruled that the Defense of Marriage Act was unconstitutional.

The Tea Party might still not have the numbers to replace or take over the Republican Party, but it was on a path to become a powerful interest group in national politics—the MoveOn of the right, as Jennifer Stefano had sought in 2008, and as Matt Kibbe had envisioned FreedomWorks becoming. Jenny Beth Martin of Tea Party Patriots said she liked the MoveOn model, as long as the Tea Party remained faithful to the grassroots, the local groups she talked to in her weekly Monday night conference calls.

"So many people are excited about the mundane, day-to-day aspects of legislation and politics," she said. "That's important. We have to hold elected officials accountable. Now people are paying attention, so they are accountable. If the Republicans take over, it doesn't mean we go back home. We continue even harder to see that the newly elected people keep their promises. That did not happen in 1994 and 2000."

If Republicans were to win a majority in Congress in

2010—or win the White House in 2012—the Tea Partiers might keep the party from drinking what Dick Armey called "backsliders' wine" when it came to spending and pork-barrel projects. They might push for means testing or raising the age of eligibility for Social Security and Medicare, if the libertarian wing of the movement could sway the older beneficiaries of these programs who filled the rallies. They might run primary challengers against lawmakers they did not consider fiscally conservative, just as MoveOn had backed challengers to two incumbent Democratic senators, Blanche Lincoln of Arkansas (who won) and Arlen Specter of Pennsylvania (who lost).

But if American history is a guide, there had never been much public support for the solutions advanced in the pure Tea Party ideology. The things the Tea Partiers advocated were not new; it was just that no one had ever been able to get a winning coalition behind them. Barry Goldwater had pledged fealty to a small-government vision of the Constitution in 1964, but as much energy as he inspired, the conservative movement did not win the White House until sixteen years later, after it had added social conservatives to its coalition. And the deficit and the debt soared under Ronald Reagan.

But if the Tea Party might never run things, it was never going to be defeated, either, because just as there would always be big government in America, there would always be a vocal opposition to big government.

When Brendan Steinhauser began working at Freedom-Works, one of the first books he read was *Armey's Axioms*, the collection of his new boss's favorite aphorisms. The axiom governing the last chapter was "Washington is a city of young idealists and old cynics." You stayed young and idealistic, Armey argued, as long as you didn't care about fitting in, as long as you didn't sell your soul to be part of the action.

As he planned for his second 9/12 march in the summer of 2010, Steinhauser called himself "realistically idealistic."

"I fight the good fight and have fun doing it," he said. "I don't think I'm cynical yet. You're going to win some battles and lose some battles."

The men and women of the Tea Party, this coalition of young and old, were the new young idealists in town. As the 2010 midterms approached, they would be faced with reality: Would they keep pushing for ideals that had been beating against the march of the nation's history for decades? Or would they support people who made compromises that would still get them closer to their goals on spending?

Washington was also a city of endless compromises, as Rand Paul's favorite Rush lyric had it. But if that would turn the Tea Partiers into old cynics, it was no cause for concern. Young idealists were more than just part of the fabric of Washington; they were part of the fabric of American politics, and had been for more than two hundred years. The Tea Partiers of today might one day become cynical, they might one day be co-opted. But even if that happened, history argued that a new generation of young idealists would be back soon.

Afterword

The Tea Party set the agenda for the 2010 midterm elections.

In exit polls on election day, a remarkable four in ten voters described themselves as Tea Party supporters. Forty-seven candidates running on a Tea Party platform were elected to the House of Representatives, and five to the Senate. In all, 138 candidates for congressional offices ran on a Tea Party platform—meaning there was a Tea Party candidate for more than half the seats that were open or held by Democrats in the House, and a third of those in the Senate.

The Tea Party was responsible for electing more than half the freshman class in the House—with eighty-seven members, it was the largest new class in sixty years, far bigger than the one produced by the last Republican revolution in 1994. It was not just a wave election, but—to use the phrase Rand Paul repeated in his victory speech when he won the Senate election in Kentucky—"a Tea Party tidal wave." President Obama himself called it a "shellacking" in his news conference after the results were in. It was a stunning show of power for a movement that eighteen months earlier had consisted of little more than Keli Carender's portable amplifier and some home-made signs. The Tea Party had given the Republican Party an unexpected rebirth after its crushing defeats in the Democratic sweep of Congress in 2006 and in the presidential race of 2008.

The question throughout the 2010 campaign had been whether the Tea Party would hurt or help Republicans. By nominating untested candidates over more certain establishment figures in Republican primaries, would Tea Party voters ultimately hand seats to the Democrats? Or would the sheer passion of the Tea Party carry the day?

In the Senate races, the Tea Party proved more of a liability than an asset. Republicans lost three seats to Democrats in races where Tea Party candidates had won the primaries—narrowly denying the party the Senate majority that had seemed so within its grasp just a few months earlier.

In Nevada, Sharron Angle lost to Harry Reid, the Senate majority leader, the candidate Republicans most dearly wanted to beat and the one Democrats most feared could lose. Angle hurt herself with off-the-wall comments—asserting erroneously that Dearborn, Michigan, a largely Arab-American community, was ruled by Sharia law; and telling Hispanic students that they looked "a little more Asian to me." She fled from reporters, finally explaining to a Fox News interviewer that she thought the role of the media was to ask only the questions that she wanted to answer.

Most frustrating to Republicans was the candidacy of Christine O'Donnell, the party's nominee for the open U.S. Senate seat in Delaware. She was a perennial candidate with a history of financial problems, and even national Tea Party groups like FreedomWorks did not support her in the Republican primary, preferring her opponent, Representative Michael N. Castle. Though Castle was a moderate, he was also the clear favorite to win the seat for the Republicans in the general election, having been elected to statewide office more than ten times. But passionate local groups campaigned fervently for O'Donnell, and the Tea Party Express delivered an infusion of cash in the waning days of the primary, as it had done for Scott Brown in Massachusetts. The Tea Party passion was sufficient to carry O'Donnell to victory in the primary but not nearly enough in the general election. O'Donnell was also hurt by intense media attention to bizarre statements she had made in interviews from the 1990s, including, notably, an assertion that she had "dabbled" in witchcraft. Such statements, broadcast widely, proved too alienating for moderate voters, and the Democrats retained the seat.

In Alaska, the incumbent, Senator Lisa Murkowski, refused to drop out of the race after a Tea Party candidate named Joe Miller beat her in the Republican primary. Murkowski had long been at odds with Sarah Palin, a dislike born of the bitter 2006 governor's race, when Palin unseated Murkowski's father, Frank Murkowski. She campaigned as the un-Palin, arguing the benefits of big government—an understandable tactic for an Alaskan, given the state's reliance on federal largess, but an unusual one for a Republican in 2010. Murkowski won handily on a write-in bid, something that only one other U.S. senator, Strom Thurmond, had done before.

Still, Rand Paul won in Kentucky, helped mostly by stumbles by his Democratic opponent, who turned off voters by focusing largely on revelations about Paul's fraternity pranks in college. Pat Toomey was elected in Pennsylvania, and in Wisconsin Ron Johnson, a plastics magnate who said that he was inspired to enter politics after speaking about health care

at a Tea Party meeting, ousted Russell Feingold, a three-term
senator and a liberal mainstay of the Democratic Party.

In the House races, a Tea Party affiliation was an undeni-
able advantage. Some Tea Party candidates won in districts
that had long favored Republicans, but there were surprises,
too—Tea Party candidates won almost every toss-up race,
including some in districts where Democrats had been favored.
They won despite Democratic efforts to paint them as extrem-
ists; several Tea Party candidates pledged to repeal the Sixteenth and Seventeenth Amendments and eliminate wide
swaths of federal government—the departments of energy,
education, and commerce—and some even called for an end
to Social Security, the third rail of modern American politics.
(Steve Stivers, a candidate from Ohio who had lost a bid for a
House seat in 2008 but won in 2010 by moving to the right,
campaigned on a pledge to get rid of all federal departments
except state, defense, justice, and the treasury.)

They won despite making outrageous comments—Allen
West, running to represent Florida's Twenty-second District,
exhorted his supporters to "get your musket, fix your bayo-
net," and make his Democratic opponent "scared to come out
of his house." West, a former Army lieutenant colonel who
had resigned after an investigation into his conduct during the
interrogation of a detainee, had also run in 2008 and lost. A
black conservative, he became a Tea Party rock star in 2010,
raising more money than any House challenger, and won by
a comfortable margin.

And many Tea Party candidates won despite allegations of
financial improprieties. In a House district north and west of
Chicago, another repeat candidate named Joe Walsh had won
the primary in February 2010 and appeared at the Tea Party
convention that month pledging not to abandon his Tea Party

values as he campaigned in the general election. Three months later, his top campaign staff quit after revelations that Walsh had lost a home to foreclosure, and accusations that he had failed to pay federal and state taxes, and had been cited several times for driving without a license or insurance. Local Republican leaders considered replacing him, and national Democrats, with so many other races to fight across the country, figured that this was one they could count on winning. But Walsh won—if only by 291 votes, the narrowest margin of any House candidate.

The House candidates probably benefitted from less media attention, but on some level, voters may not have cared even if they had heard more about them. It was a change election, as the elections of 2006 and 2008 had been—except that exit polls found that voters were even more dissatisfied with Congress than they had been in the midterms of 2006, when the wave brought in the Democrats. This time, the incumbents being tossed out were many of those same Democrats who had been the previous agents of change.

"We've come to take our government back," Rand Paul told jubilant supporters who gathered in Bowling Green on election night. "They say that the U.S. Senate is the world's most deliberative body. I'm going to ask them to deliberate on this: The American people are unhappy with what's going on in Washington."

~

Being unhappy was the easy part. It was one thing to have a party, another to deal with the morning after.

The Tea Party was still not an official party, and remained less a movement than a state of mind—relatively few people who had voted for Tea Party candidates had ever been to a

Tea Party rally or meeting. Candidates appealed to that state of mind by running on generally vague platforms: the health care legislation now derided as Obamacare was bad, the Constitution was good, Congress could not be trusted with the taxpayers' money. It wasn't clear what the Tea Party's mandate was, or even what had swayed voters in the end, beyond a sense that government was at once too remote and too intrusive, and too disconnected from their values. They were driven more by outrage than ideology, more by pique than by policy.

It did not take long after the election for it to become clear that no one could agree on what the Tea Party victory meant.

Republican congressional candidates had paid homage to the Tea Party in their campaign manifesto, the "Pledge to America," and the newly elected representatives did so again in the rules they adopted when the 112th Congress was sworn in. Lawmakers, led by John Boehner, the new speaker of the House, staged a reading of the Constitution on the House floor as one of their first official acts. And new rules required that all bills indicate the specific provision of the Constitution that authorized such legislation—a promise lifted from the Contract from America, the Tea Party's own manifesto.

The Republicans had also made a pitch for Tea Party votes by vowing to cut $100 billion from the 2011 federal budget. But once in the majority, it turned out that $100 billion didn't really mean $100 billion—it was more like $35 billion, which Republicans argued would have been equivalent to $74 billion if the budget had been for a full year instead of the seven months remaining in the fiscal year. This accounting sleight of hand did not satisfy the Tea Party freshmen or the Democrats, both of whom pointed out that the Republicans had known when they made their initial pledge that the budget was only for the remaining portion of the year.

The Tea Party freshmen asserted themselves in the Republican caucus, forcing the party's leaders to declare that they would eliminate the entire $100 billion. Some Republicans complained that this would cut into the bones of many necessary programs—housing, energy, environment, transportation—and completely eliminate more than sixty federal programs altogether.

As the Democrats resisted these demands, Tea Party supporters urged a government shutdown to make their point. "We will prevail," declared Michele Bachmann, the founder of the new Tea Party caucus in the House. She spoke at a Tea Party rally on the East Lawn of the Capitol on a chilly afternoon in April, as about two hundred people cheered, carrying signs declaring, SHUTDOWN OKAY, STATUS QUO, NO WAY and BOEHNER, GET A BACKBONE.

Perhaps inevitably, a last-minute deal on April 8 avoided a shutdown. But that still left more complicated budget fights—over the 2012 federal budget and the question of raising the debt ceiling, the limit on the amount of money the country can legally borrow.

The new mood of Tea Party austerity had made a celebrity of Paul Ryan, a forty-year-old congressman from southeastern Wisconsin. In 2008, he had proposed a "Roadmap for America," a budget plan that he introduced by quoting Friedrich Hayek on the perils heading down "the road to serfdom." It proposed massive changes to the entitlement programs at the crux of the nation's debt. For people younger than fifty-five, Medicare would be changed, from a system that paid medical bills directly to one that provided vouchers to help purchase health insurance, and Social Security benefits would be invested in private savings accounts, with means testing for benefits and an increase in the retirement age. In keeping with the free-market spirit of the Tea Party libertarians, the "roadmap" also proposed replacing the corporate income tax with an 8.5 percent consumption tax and reducing tax rates on the wealthiest Americans.

In 2008, Republicans had kept their distance from Ryan's proposals, aware that few candidates won elections by pledging to change Medicare or Social Security. But by 2011, Ryan had ascended to new power—he was the incoming chairman of the House Budget Committee, and under the Republican rules adopted after the 2010 election, he had the power to unilaterally set a ceiling on the federal budget. In January he delivered the Republican response to the president's State of the Union address. And his roadmap became a model for many Tea Party supporters within the Republican Party.

With the Tea Party influence in the new Congress, Ryan's plan became the basis for the budget that passed the House of Representatives in April 2011. It was unlikely to become law—the Senate was still controlled by Democrats, and President Obama would surely veto it. Still, Republicans held it up as evidence that they were once again the party of fiscal discipline.

Yet when new Tea Party representatives returned to their districts for Easter recess, they found themselves confronted by the kind of angry protests over health care that had greeted the Democrats in the summer of 2009. Only this time, constituents were fearful or furious over the Ryan plan for Medicare. Several meetings became so contentious that police had to remove protesters. Ryan himself was booed as he outlined the plan in his own district.

Americans could also look elsewhere to see the results of

all the Tea Party fury—and they didn't always like what they saw. In Wisconsin, Scott Walker, the new Republican governor (whose 2010 campaign had been supported by the libertarian group Americans for Prosperity), worked with a new Republican majority in the legislature to pass a bill that would all but eliminate collective-bargaining rights for state employees and would also curtail the power of the unions by eliminating mandatory dues. Thousands of protesters descended on the state capitol in Madison in the weeks that followed his proposal, camping out under the dome, and marching, dancing, and drumming in protest for weeks.

In the protest lines, some state employees said that they had voted for Walker because he had promised not to build a high-speed rail line that they considered a waste of money. They expected him to balance the budget, not take away their unions' right to negotiate how many hours they had to work, or whether they could take time off to care for a sick parent.

Even in the face of all this turmoil, however, the Tea Party sentiment had not died down.

It was perhaps most enduring in local tax revolts, as blocs of angry voters turned out to reject tax increases and demand cuts to municipal and state budgets. Democrats as well as Republicans were moved by this popular sentiment—in New York, the new governor, Andrew Cuomo, who had easily defeated the Tea Party candidate who had won the Republican primary for governor, led the legislature in pushing for a 2 percent cap on property taxes that was reminiscent of those in California and Massachusetts during the early years of the Reagan era.

Activists were also preparing primary challenges to longtime moderate Republican senators, like Olympia Snowe in Maine, and also to those who under most pre-Tea Party definitions would have been considered conservatives: Orrin Hatch in Utah and Richard Lugar in Indiana.

On a Saturday evening in April 2011, Senator Lugar spoke to a crowd of about 125 people at the Clay County Republican Club in Brazil, Indiana. In remarks he had been repeating across the state, he talked about Republicans who wanted to vote against raising the debt ceiling, who believed that the United States could simply stop borrowing money and live with whatever budget chaos ensued. Before he could get to the part where he called this irresponsible, the crowd cut him off and began applauding loudly.

"Well, some are in agreement," Lugar said, looking somewhat surprised.

One by one, people who were supporting his Tea Party challenger in the primary got up to question him. "We're borrowing about a third of what we take in every year," said a sixty-four-year-old homemaker named Judy Proctor. "That is insane. No country has ever in the history of the world done that and not ended up bankrupt."

"China doesn't want to lend us money, Canada doesn't want to lend, we're obviously irresponsible," she continued, her voice rising and almost breaking. "Then we have Senator Lugar saying, 'Well, maybe we can make it a little better next year. Maybe after that we can make it a little more better.' It's not enough. We have to stop. A third of our budget is borrowed! If we don't do something dramatic, and soon, we're done. And it may already be too late."

Another man got up to demand that Lugar reassure him that his personal share of the national debt—less than $3,000 when Mr. Lugar entered office thirty-five years earlier—would not hit $50,000.

"I can't," Lugar replied candidly. "I'm simply saying I can

work with members of the Republican Party in support of
what they are doing, and convincing enough Democrats to
actually make progress in this area, as opposed to giving
speeches about it or endless rhetoric or waving my hands about
how horrible it all is."

It was a familiar Tea Party story: a six-term veteran of the
Senate, a foreign policy expert with connections around the
world, a champion for conservative causes like a balanced
budget amendment and ending farm subsidies, suddenly finding himself in trouble. Just six years earlier, he had been so
well liked in the state that the Democrats had declined to
challenge him. Now, plenty of voters seemed unimpressed by
his experience. "We're in a crisis," said Katelyn Burk, a twenty-
year-old Tea Party supporter. "We need new people. Obviously, stability is not working."

The Republican Party was still in an identity crisis, and so was
the Tea Party. The confusion carried over into the early stages
of the 2012 presidential race. On the one hand, the Tea Party
had changed the field. That Michele Bachmann could be considered a credible potential candidate was a testament to the
power of the Tea Party. Ron Paul, likewise, got into the race,
believing that his economic message would carry even more
resonance this time around. (Rand Paul had said that if his
father didn't run, he would.)

At the Tea Party Patriots Convention in Phoenix in Feb-
ruary 2011, a straw poll found that the favored candidate was
Herman Cain, the former chief executive of Godfather's Pizza
and a talk radio host in Atlanta, who liked to tell interviewers,
"I was talking to Tea Parties before it was cool." Jenny Beth
Martin of Tea Party Patriots said Tea Party audiences loved

him. "He doesn't have a title before his name," she explained. "He's not a senator or a governor, he's just a mister." Sarah Palin made a show of teasing reporters and the public about whether she would run, but she was clear about one thing, telling Sean Hannity, "I want to make sure that we have a candidate out there with Tea Party principles." Her remarks made plain how much Republican presidential candidates felt the need to wrap themselves in the Tea Party mantle. Tim Pawlenty, the former governor of Minnesota, who was often called T-Paw, began his campaign trying to brand himself as "TeaPaw."

But it wasn't clear that Palin was the Tea Party favorite—or that anyone was. By the spring of 2011, there was no Republican front-runner—a situation that had occurred only twice since 1952: in 1964 when Barry Goldwater emerged late, and in 2008, when John McCain did. It was striking that a movement that had had so much influence in the congressional races a few months earlier could be displaying so little firmness in the presidential race.

And presidential elections typically draw a younger and more diverse set of voters—the sorts of voters who had gone for Obama in 2008. The Tea Party had been a phenomenon of the midterm elections, when turnout is lower and tends to be older and whiter—to look, in other words, more like the Tea Party. Just by sheer demographics, its voice was likely to be less influential in 2012.

The Tea Party was also stuck deciding what it really stood for.

In late April, Jenny Beth Martin appeared at a forum about the Tea Party at Harvard's Kennedy School of Government. The setting suggested how establishment this former mom blogger had become. She had recently hired a Washington public-relations firm to represent her.

The moderator was none other than Trey Grayson, who had gone on to become the director of the school's Institute of Politics, following his primary loss to Rand Paul in the Republican U.S. Senate primary in Kentucky. Grayson had wanted the school to host a panel discussion on the Tea Party and felt it was important that he be the moderator, even if the topic might be personally uncomfortable.

Grayson asked relatively neutral questions of the panelists. The audience wanted more details about what the Tea Party actually wanted to achieve. An actuary who worked for the Medicare program stood up and asked how, exactly, the Tea Party intended to solve the puzzle of entitlements.

"That's not up to us," Martin replied.

Several in the audience groaned. But the Tea Party activists made no apology.

The performance was emblematic of the strange power of the Tea Party. It had changed the conversation and loomed as a threat over every Republican, but it had yet to explain what it was offering in opposition. And even Tea Party voters were not necessarily ready for the choices that their demands for fiscal discipline would require.

Nowhere was this more evident than in the debate over Medicare. By the spring of 2011, "Keep your government hands off my Medicare" had gone from an ill-informed Tea Party slogan to an urgent demand. Except that the bid by the federal government to fundamentally reshape Medicare was in the hands of the Republican majority that the Tea Party had put into power.

Democrats saw this as a wedge issue they could use to win elections. They got their first chance in late May, in a special election for a House seat in New York's Twenty-sixth District. It recalled the Tea Party's first campaign, back in November

2009—it was an upstate New York district that had long been in Republican hands, with a third party candidate making things difficult for the Republican.

But this time, the Democrat, Kathy Hochul, made the Republicans' plan to overhaul Medicare the center of her argument. The national Democratic party organizations saw her gaining traction, and supplied her with money for advertisements.

Even though a Democrat should have been a long shot to capture the seat, Hochul won. As she declared victory at a local union hall, she asked the cheering supporters, "Did we not have the right issues on our side?" The crowd chanted, "Medicare!"

As with any election, the outcome reflected local particulars: the Republican candidate had been weak while Hochul campaigned energetically. But national Republican leaders conceded that they were losing on the issue of Medicare. It was far from clear that the special election in the Twenty-sixth District was a harbinger of a swing toward the Democrats. But the results did argue that the Tea Party's desire for austerity was not as strong among the general public as the results of the 2010 midterm elections had suggested.

The day after the election, Democrats in the Senate forced a vote on the Ryan budget, hoping to put Republicans on the defensive and sending a message that they intended to make it the center of their campaign in 2012. The budget failed, predictably. Less predictable was the division within the Republican ranks. Five Republican senators opposed the Ryan budget. One, Rand Paul, did so because he argued it did not go far enough. Two northeastern moderates, Olympia Snowe and Susan Collins of Maine, voted against it. So did Lisa Murkowski, who had triumphed over the Tea Party in November. And so did Scott Brown, the man who just eighteen months earlier had been the very symbol of Tea Party potency.

Republicans responded by calling a vote of their own, on whether to raise the debt ceiling. They won—again, predictably. The debt-ceiling increase was shot down.

The vote was largely symbolic. But the debate over the debt ceiling continued well into the summer swelter in Washington, becoming increasingly acrimonious as the date approached when a refusal to raise the limit would result in the government defaulting on its loans. It was impossible not to see the influence of the Tea Party. Speaker Boehner walked away from negotiations with the White House and Democratic leaders several times, and even when the talks appeared to make progress, he was careful to insist before the television cameras that he had made no deal, public or private. He was mindful that members of the Tea Party caucus, led by Michele Bachmann, had declared that they would refuse any increase in the debt limit. And with the 2010 elections still fresh in their minds— and another election little more than a year away—Republicans did not want to be seen as compromising with Democrats. The party had embraced a hard Tea Party position, insisting on deep spending cuts and no tax increases. It limited the Republicans' negotiating room: Even the closing of a tax loophole would be portrayed as a tax hike.

It was an article of faith in Washington that the two parties would have to reach an agreement, as establishment Republicans would not want to be held responsible for the collapse of the financial markets likely to result from the United States defaulting on its debts. But newly elected Tea Party Republicans, faced with the realities of governing, were already hearing rumblings of primary challenges back in their districts. The anger and impatience that had helped elect them was still fresh, only now it was turned on them.

And so, two and a half years after the inauguration of Barack Obama and the emergence of the Tea Party movement, with the country still struggling to emerge from its great recession, the tussle continued unresolved: Democrat versus Republican, moderate versus conservative, the promise of change versus the promise of change.

New York Times/CBS News Poll of Tea Party Supporters

This appendix contains the results of a *New York Times*/CBS News poll conducted in April 2010, which included an over-sample of Tea Party supporters.

The *New York Times*/CBS News poll was based on telephone interviews conducted April 5, 2010, through April 12, 2010, with 1,580 adults throughout the United States, including 881 who said they were "supporters of the Tea Party movement."

The sample of landline telephone exchanges called was randomly selected by a computer from a complete list of more than 69,000 active residential exchanges across the country. The exchanges were chosen so as to ensure that each region of the country was represented in proportion to its population.

Within each exchange, random digits were added to form a complete telephone number, thus permitting access to listed and unlisted numbers alike. Within each household, one adult was designated by a random procedure to be the respondent.

To increase coverage, this landline sample was supplemented by respondents reached through random dialing of cell phone numbers. The two samples were then combined.

Interviewers made multiple efforts to reach every phone number in the survey, calling back unanswered numbers on different days at different times of both day and evening.

For purposes of analysis, people who said they supported the Tea Party movement were oversampled in this poll. Several thousand random phone numbers were screened for Tea Party supporters and qualifying adults were interviewed as part of the April 2010 national poll, along with callbacks to Tea Party supporters from a February 2010 poll, yielding a total of 881 respondents. They were weighted to their proper proportion of the population (about 18 percent) as determined in the February and April surveys.

The combined results have been weighted to adjust for variation in the sample relating to geographic area, sex, race, Hispanic origin, marital status, age, education, and number of adults in the household. In addition, the landline respondents were weighted to take into account the number of telephone lines into the residence, while the cell phone respondents were weighted according to whether they were reachable only by cell phone or also by landline.

In theory, in nineteen cases out of twenty, results based on such samples of all adults will differ by no more than three percentage points in either direction from what would have been obtained by seeking to interview all American adults. For the oversample of Tea Party supporters, it is also plus or minus three percentage points. For smaller subgroups, like the most activist supporters, the margin of sampling error is larger. Shifts in results between polls over time also have a larger sampling error.

In addition to sampling error, the practical difficulties of conducting any survey of public opinion may introduce other sources of error into the poll. Variation in the wording and order of questions, for example, may lead to somewhat different results.

Complete questions and results are available at nytimes.com/polls.

1. Do you approve or disapprove of the way Barack Obama is handling his job as president?

	Approve	Disapprove	DK/NA
All Respondents	50	40	10
Tea Party Supporters	7	88	5

2. Regardless of your overall opinion of him, what do you like BEST about Barack Obama? (Questions 2–3 were rotated.)

	All Respondents	Tea Party Supporters
Economic policy/making economy better	1	
Health care reform/laws	8	–
Changing Washington	2	–
Bringing people together	1	
Understands my needs and problems/working for me	2	
More openness in government	–	
Accomplishing a lot/Working hard	5	2
First black president	1	1
Family values/morals	3	1
His wife and family	3	6
Intelligent	3	2
Communicator	6	11
Education policy	1	–
Like his policies (general)	2	–
Afghanistan policy	–	1
Foreign policy (general)	1	–
Like him (general)	20	19
Everything	–	
Nothing	7	16
Other	8	12
DK/NA	26	29

3. Regardless of your overall opinion, what do you like LEAST about Barack Obama? (Questions 2–3 were rotated.)

	All Respondents	Tea Party Supporters
Economic policy/not improving the economy	2	4
Health care reform/law	10	10
Not being bipartisan/not working with Republicans	1	1
Trying to be too bipartisan	3	
Expanding government	1	3
Tax policy/taxes increases	1	1
Education policy	1	
Afghanistan policy	1	–
Plans for Guantanamo Bay	1	
Abortion stance	1	–
Not working hard	1	–
Too liberal/not conservative enough	2	3
Spending too much money	2	5
Increasing the deficit/debt	–	1
Socialist/Turning U.S. into socialist country	2	11
Immigration	1	–
Dishonest	4	9
He's Muslim	1	1
Making the U.S. less safe/soft on terrorism	–	1
Don't like his cabinet	–	1
Lack of values	–	1
Don't like his policies (general)	2	5
Foreign policy (general)	1	1
Don't like him (general)	10	19
Everything	1	1
Nothing	6	2
Other	8	13
DK/NA	36	7

4. Do you feel things in this country are generally going in the right direction or do you feel things have pretty seriously gotten off on the wrong track?

	Right	Wrong	DK/NA
All Respondents	34	59	7
Tea Party Supporters	6	92	2

5. What do you think is the most important problem facing the country today?

	All Respondents	Tea Party Supporters
Health Care	8	4
Social Security	–	
Budget Deficit	5	11
Education	1	1
Medicare/Medicaid	–	
Taxes	–	1
Economy	23	23
Immigration	1	1
Defense	1	3
Poverty	4	–
Crime	–	
Foreign Policy	–	–
Jobs	27	22
Abortion	1	1
Moral Values	2	2
Welfare	–	
President	–	1
War	1	1
Iraq	2	
Afghanistan	1	
Politicians/Government	4	13
Heating Oil/Gas	–	
Environment	1	1
Religious Values	1	3

	All Respondents	Tea Party Supporters
Terrorism general	1	1
Other	11	10
DK/NA	5	1

6. Do you approve or disapprove of the way Barack Obama is handling the economy?

	Approve	Disapprove	DK/NA
All Respondents	43	46	11
Tea Party Supporters	6	91	3

7. Do you approve or disapprove of the way Barack Obama is handling health care?

	Approve	Disapprove	DK/NA
All Respondents	41	51	9
Tea Party Supporters	6	93	2

8. Do you approve or disapprove of the way Barack Obama is handling the federal budget deficit?

	Approve	Disapprove	DK/NA
All Respondents	29	53	18
Tea Party Supporters	5	91	4

9. Do you approve or disapprove of the way Congress is handling its job?

	Approve	Disapprove	DK/NA
All Respondents	17	73	10
Tea Party Supporters	1	96	3

10. How about the representative in Congress from your district? Do you approve or disapprove of the way your representative is handling his or her job?

	Approve	Disapprove	DK/NA
All Respondents	46	36	18
Tea Party Supporters	40	49	10

11. Do you think most members of Congress have done a good enough job to deserve reelection, or do you think it's time to give new people a chance?

	Deserve reelection	Time for new people	Depends (vol.)	DK/NA
All Respondents	10	78	7	5
Tea Party Supporters	1	94	4	1

12. Is your opinion of Barack Obama favorable, not favorable, undecided, or haven't you heard enough about Barack Obama yet to have an opinion?

	Favorable	Not favorable	Undecided	Haven't heard enough	Refused
All Respondents	43	33	17	7	1
Tea Party Supporters	7	84	7	1	–

13. How would you rate the condition of the national economy these days? Is it very good, fairly good, fairly bad, or very bad?

	Very good	Fairly good	Fairly bad	Very bad	DK/NA
All Respondents	1	22	43	34	1
Tea Party Supporters	–	6	39	54	1

14. Do you think the economy is getting better, getting worse, or staying about the same?

	Better	Worse	Same	DK/NA
All Respondents	33	23	43	1
Tea Party Supporters	14	42	42	1

[There is no question 15.]

16. When it comes to the availability of good jobs for American workers, some say that America's best years are behind us. Others say that the best times are yet to come. What do you think?

	Best years behind	Best yet to come	DK/NA
All Respondents	45	45	10
Tea Party Supporters	58	33	9

17. Who do you think is mostly to blame for the current state of the nation's economy—1. the Bush administration, 2. the Obama administration, 3. Wall Street and financial institutions, 4. Congress, or 5. someone else? (Answer options were rotated.)

	All Respondents	Tea Party Supporters
Bush administration	32	5
Obama administration	4	10
Wall Street and financial institutions	22	15
Congress	10	28
Someone else	7	6
All of the above (vol.)	9	15
Combination (vol.)	13	20
DK/NA	2	1

18. So far, do you think the federal government's stimulus package has made the economy better, made the economy worse, or has it had no impact on the economy so far?

	Better	Worse	No impact	DK/NA
All Respondents	32	18	44	6
Tea Party Supporters	10	36	52	2

[There is no question 19.]

20. Some people say the country needs a third political party—a new party to compete with the Democratic and Republican parties. Do you agree or disagree?

	Agree	Disagree	DK/NA
All Respondents	46	48	6
Tea Party Supporters	40	52	8

21. How much of the time do you think you can trust the government in Washington to do what is right—just about always, most of the time, or only some of the time?

	Always	Most	Some	Never (vol.)	DK/NA
All Respondents	4	16	70	8	2
Tea Party Supporters		6	75	19	–

22. If you had to choose, would you rather have a smaller government providing fewer services, or a bigger government providing more services?

	Smaller	Bigger	Depends (vol.)	DK/NA
All Respondents	50	37	5	8
Tea Party Supporters	92	4	2	2

23. Suppose a smaller government required cuts in spending on domestic programs such as Social Security, Medicare, education, or defense—then would you favor a smaller government, or not? (Based on those who answered "smaller" to question 22.)

	Favor	Not favor	DK/NA
All Respondents	58	36	6
Tea Party Supporters	73	20	7

24. Which comes closest to your feelings about the way things are going in Washington—enthusiastic, satisfied but not enthusiastic, dissatisfied but not angry, or angry?

	Enthusiastic	Satisfied but not enthusiastic	Dissatisfied but not angry	Angry	DK/NA
All Respondents	5	26	48	19	2
Tea Party Supporters	1	4	41	53	–

25. What are you most angry about? (Based on those who answered "angry" to question 24.)

	All Respondents	Tea Party Supporters
Size of government/increased role of government	3	6
Government spending	9	11
Barack Obama/Obama administration	5	6
Socialist policies	3	2
Taxes	1	2
Federal budget deficit	4	5
Health care reform	14	16
Bank bailout/TARP	2	1
Wall Street/Banks	–	–
Partisan politics/Politicians	10	5
Congress	6	6
Democrats	–	–
Republicans	1	
Unemployment	7	8
Illegal immigration	–	1
Abortion	–	1
Not doing anything for me	3	3
Corruption	3	3
Not representing the people	15	14
Economy	–	1

	All Respondents	Tea Party Supporters
Other	10	8
Everything	2	–
DK/NA	2	1

26. As you may know, the budget deficit is the shortfall when the amount of money the government spends is more than the amount of money it takes in. How much have you heard or read about the federal government's current budget deficit—a lot, some, not much, or nothing at all?

	A lot	Some	Not much	Nothing at all	DK/NA
All Respondents	30	40	21	8	1
Tea Party Supporters	62	29	8	1	–

27. Which comes closer to your own view? The federal government should spend money to create jobs, even if it means increasing the budget deficit, OR the federal government should NOT spend money to create jobs and should instead focus on reducing the budget deficit.

	Create jobs	Reduce budget deficit	DK/NA
All Respondents	50	42	7
Tea Party Supporters	17	76	7

28. If you had to choose, would you prefer reducing the federal budget deficit or cutting taxes?

	Reducing deficit	Cutting taxes	DK/NA
All Respondents	45	47	8
Tea Party Supporters	42	49	9

29. Who do you think is mostly to blame for most of the current federal budget deficit—1. the Bush administration, 2. the Obama administration, 3. Congress, or 4. someone else? (Answer options were rotated.)

	All Respondents	Tea Party Supporters
Bush administration	39	6
Obama administration	8	24
Congress	19	37
Someone else	13	5
All of the above (vol.)	8	10
Combination (vol.)	9	16
DK/NA	3	1

30. Do you think providing government money to banks and other financial institutions was necessary to get the economy out of recession, or would the economy probably have improved without doing that?

	Necessary	Economy will improve without it	DK/NA
All Respondents	39	51	10
Tea Party Supporters	17	74	9

[There is no question 31.]

32. In general, is your opinion of the Republican Party favorable or not favorable? (Questions 32–33 were rotated.)

	Favorable	Not favorable	DK/NA
All Respondents	38	53	9
Tea Party Supporters	54	43	4

33. In general, is your opinion of the Democratic Party favorable or not favorable? (Questions 32–33 were rotated.)

	Favorable	Not favorable	DK/NA
All Respondents	42	50	8
Tea Party Supporters	6	92	2

34. Which political figure in the United States living TODAY do you admire most?

	All Respondents	Tea Party Supporters
Barack Obama	16	2
Bill Clinton	9	2
Hillary Clinton	3	–
Jimmy Carter	3	2
Sarah Palin	3	9
George W. Bush	2	5
George H. W. Bush	2	3
John McCain	2	3
Newt Gingrich	3	10
Mike Huckabee	1	3
Ron Paul	1	3
Mitt Romney	1	5
Rick Perry	1	–
John Boehner	–	1
Michele Bachmann	–	1
Scott Brown	–	1
Glenn Beck	–	1
Other	13	20
No one	4	5
DK/NA	36	24

35. Is your opinion of John McCain favorable, not favorable, undecided, or haven't you heard enough about John McCain yet to have an opinion?

	Favorable	Not favorable	Undecided	Haven't heard enough	Refused
All Respondents	23	36	27	12	2
Tea Party Supporters	35	37	24	3	–

36. Is your opinion of George W. Bush favorable, not favorable, undecided, or haven't you heard enough about George W. Bush yet to have an opinion?

	Favorable	Not favorable	Undecided	Haven't heard enough	Refused
All Respondents	27	58	14	1	1
Tea Party Supporters	57	27	14	1	1

37. Is your opinion of Ron Paul favorable, not favorable, undecided, or haven't you heard enough about Ron Paul yet to have an opinion?

	Favorable	Not favorable	Undecided	Haven't heard enough	Refused
All Respondents	11	12	17	59	1
Tea Party Supporters	28	15	20	36	1

38. Is your opinion of Glenn Beck favorable, not favorable, undecided, or haven't you heard enough about Glenn Beck yet to have an opinion?

	Favorable	Not favorable	Undecided	Haven't heard enough	Refused
All Respondents	18	17	17	47	1
Tea Party Supporters	59	6	17	17	–

39. Is your opinion of Sarah Palin favorable, not favorable, undecided, or haven't you heard enough about Sarah Palin yet to have an opinion?

	Favorable	Not favorable	Undecided	Haven't heard enough	Refused
All Respondents	30	45	17	7	–
Tea Party Supporters	66	12	19	2	–

40. Do you think Sarah Palin would have the ability to be an effective president, or not?

	Yes	No	DK/NA
All Respondents	26	63	11
Tea Party Supporters	40	47	13

41. How much have you heard or read about the Federal Reserve—a lot, some, not much, or nothing at all?

	A lot	Some	Not much	Nothing	DK/NA
All Respondents	17	33	37	12	–
Tea Party Supporters	25	45	25	5	1

42. How much confidence do you have in the Federal Reserve's ability to promote financial stability—a lot, some, not much, or none at all, or don't you know enough about the Federal Reserve to say?

	A lot	Some	Not much	None	Don't know enough	DK/NA
All Respondents	8	31	19	6	33	2
Tea Party Supporters	5	38	28	9	20	1

43. In trying to solve the economic problems facing the country, do you think Barack Obama has expanded the role of government too much, not enough, or about the right amount?

	Too much	Not enough	About right	DK/NA
All Respondents	37	18	36	9
Tea Party Supporters	89	3	6	2

[There is no question 44 or 45.]

46. Do you think Barack Obama does or does not understand the needs and problems of people like yourself?

	Yes	No	DK/NA
All Respondents	58	39	2
Tea Party Supporters	24	73	3

47. Do you think Barack Obama shares the values most Americans try to live by, or doesn't he?

	Yes	No	DK/NA
All Respondents	57	37	5
Tea Party Supporters	20	75	4

48. Do you think of Barack Obama as more of a liberal, a moderate, or a conservative? IF LIBERAL, ASK: Would you say he is very liberal or only somewhat liberal? IF CONSERVATIVE, ASK: Would you say he is only somewhat conservative or very conservative?

	Very liberal	Somewhat liberal	Moderate	Somewhat conservative	Very conservative	DK/NA
All Respondents	31	18	28	6	4	13
Tea Party Supporters	77	9	7	–	1	5

49. Some people say Barack Obama's policies are moving the country more toward socialism. Do you think Barack Obama's policies are moving the country more toward socialism, or are his policies not moving the country in that direction?

	Toward socialism	Not toward socialism	DK/NA
All Respondents	52	38	10
Tea Party Supporters	92	6	2

50. According to the Constitution, American presidents must be "natural born citizens." Some people say Barack Obama was NOT born in the United States, but was born in another country. Do YOU think Barack Obama was born in the United States, or was he born in another country?

	Born in US	Another country	DK/NA
All Respondents	58	20	23
Tea Party Supporters	41	30	29

51. In general, do you think the policies of the Obama administration favor the rich, favor the middle class, favor the poor, or do they treat all groups equally?

	Favor rich	Favor middle class	Favor poor	Treat equally	DK/NA
All Respondents	17	19	27	27	9
Tea Party Supporters	16	6	56	9	13

52. In general, do you think the policies of the Obama administration favor whites over blacks, favor blacks over whites, or do they treat both groups the same?

	Favor whites over blacks	Favor blacks over whites	Treat both the same	DK/NA
All Respondents	2	11	83	5
Tea Party Supporters	1	25	65	9

53. So far, do you think the Obama administration has increased taxes for most Americans, decreased taxes for most Americans, or have they kept taxes the same for most Americans?

	Increased	Decreased	Kept the same	DK/NA
All Respondents	34	10	48	9
Tea Party Supporters	64	2	30	4

54. On average, about what percentage of their household incomes would you guess most Americans pay in federal income taxes each year—less than 10 percent, between 10 and 20 percent, between 20 and 30 percent, between 30 and 40 percent, between 40 and 50 percent, or more than 50 percent, or don't you know enough to say?

	All Respondents	Tea Party Supporters
Less than 10 percent	5	11
10–20 percent	26	25
20–30 percent	25	26
30–40 percent	10	14
40–50 percent	2	3
More than 50 percent	1	1
Don't know enough	26	15
DK/NA	5	5

55. As long as the federal government provides financial help to those who cannot afford health insurance, do you think the federal government should or should not require all Americans to have health insurance?

	Should	Should not	DK/NA
All Respondents	49	45	7
Tea Party Supporters	12	85	3

56. Do you think it is a good idea or a bad idea to raise income taxes on households that make more than $250,000 a year in order to help provide health insurance for people who do not already have it?

	Good idea	Bad idea	DK/NA
All Respondents	54	39	7
Tea Party Supporters	17	80	3

57. Do you approve or disapprove of requiring health insurance companies to cover anyone who applies for health insurance regardless of whether or not they have an existing medical condition or a prior illness?

	Approve	Disapprove	DK/NA
All Respondents	81	15	4
Tea Party Supporters	59	32	9

[There is no question 58.]

59. Overall, do you think the benefits from government programs such as Social Security and Medicare are worth the costs of those programs for taxpayers, or are they not worth the costs?

	Worth it	Not worth it	DK/NA
All Respondents	76	19	5
Tea Party Supporters	62	33	6

[There are no questions 60 and 61.]

62. Do you think providing government benefits to poor people encourages them to remain poor, or does it help them until they begin to stand on their own?

	Remain poor	Helps until they're on own	DK/NA
All Respondents	38	47	15
Tea Party Supporters	73	16	11

63. When thinking about important issues facing the country, which concerns you more right now—economic issues like taxes and jobs or social issues like abortion and same-sex marriage?

	Economic issues	Social issues	Both (vol.)	DK/NA
All Respondents	80	13	4	2
Tea Party Supporters	78	14	7	–

64. Should LEGAL immigration into the United States be kept at its present level, increased, or decreased?

	Present level	Increased	Decreased	DK/NA
All Respondents	35	16	41	7
Tea Party Supporters	39	14	42	5

65. What about ILLEGAL immigration, how serious a problem do you think the issue of ILLEGAL immigration is for the country right now—very serious, somewhat serious, not too serious, or not at all serious?

	Very	Somewhat	Not too	Not at all	DK/NA
All Respondents	60	23	12	3	2
Tea Party Supporters	82	15	2	1	1

66. Do you think global warming is an environmental problem that is causing a serious impact now, or do you think the impact of global warming won't happen until sometime in the future, or do you think global warming won't have a serious impact at all?

	Impact now	In the future	No serious impact	Doesn't exist (vol.)	DK/NA
All Respondents	38	29	24	5	3
Tea Party Supporters	12	19	51	15	3

67. Which comes closest to your view? Gay couples should be allowed to legally marry, OR gay couples should be allowed to form civil unions but not legally marry, OR there should be no legal recognition of a gay couple's relationship?

	Marry	Civil unions	No legal recognition	DK/NA
All Respondents	39	24	30	7
Tea Party Supporters	16	41	40	3

68. Which of these comes closest to your view? 1. Abortion should be generally available to those who want it; OR 2. Abortion should be available but under stricter limits than it is now; OR 3. Abortion should not be permitted?

	Available	Available but stricter	Not permitted	DK/NA
All Respondents	36	38	23	3
Tea Party Supporters	20	45	32	2

69. In general, do you think gun control laws should be made more strict, less strict, or kept as they are now?

	More	Less	Kept as they are now	DK/NA
All Respondents	40	16	42	3
Tea Party Supporters	13	30	55	2

70. In states where it is legal to openly carry a gun, should private businesses like stores and restaurants be able to prohibit customers from openly carrying guns in their establishments, or should those customers be allowed to openly carry guns into the stores and restaurants?

	Should prohibit guns	Should allow guns	Depends (vol.)	DK/NA
All Respondents	74	21	3	3
Tea Party Supporters	65	27	5	3

71. In general, who do you think has a better chance of getting ahead in today's society—white people, black people, or do white people and black people have about an equal chance of getting ahead?

	White people	Black people	Equal	DK/NA
All Respondents	31	4	60	5
Tea Party Supporters	16	7	73	4

72. In recent years, do you think too much has been made of the problems facing black people, too little has been made, or is it about right?

	Too much	Too little	Just right	DK/NA
All Respondents	28	16	44	11
Tea Party Supporters	52	6	36	6

73. When someone says the country is moving toward socialism, what does that mean to you?

	All Respondents	Tea Party Supporters
Government ownership	26	49
Getting rid of private property	1	–
Redistribution of wealth	6	8
Russia/Stalin	1	1
Communist	3	3
Giving money to the poor	1	–
Taking over businesses	1	5
Universal health care	1	1
Like Sweden	1	2
Like Cuba	1	
Bad thing	3	3
Good thing	2	–
Scare tactic	3	1
Taking rights away	6	11
Against American way	–	1
Not moving toward socialism	2	–

	All Respondents	Tea Party Supporters
Nothing	1	
Other	11	10
DK/NA	30	5

74. Do you think it is ever justified for citizens to take violent action against the government, or is it never justified?

	Justified	Never justified	DK/NA
All Respondents	16	79	5
Tea Party Supporters	24	71	5

75. More than thirty-five years ago, the Supreme Court's decision in *Roe v. Wade* established a constitutional right for women to obtain legal abortions in this country. In general, do you think the Court's decision was a good thing or a bad thing?

	Good thing	Bad thing	Both good/bad (vol.)	DK/NA
All Respondents	58	34	3	5
Tea Party Supporters	40	53	3	4

76. Do you regard the income tax which you will have to pay this year as fair, or not?

	Yes, fair	No, not fair	DK/NA
All Respondents	62	30	8
Tea Party Supporters	52	42	5

[There is no question 77.]

78. How much have you heard or read about the Tea Party movement—a lot, some, not much, or nothing at all yet?

	A lot	Some	Not much	Nothing	DK/NA
All Respondents	19	31	22	28	–
Tea Party Supporters	50	43	6	2	

79. Is your opinion of the Tea Party movement favorable, not favorable, undecided, or haven't you heard enough about the Tea Party movement yet to have an opinion?

	Favorable	Not favorable	Undecided	Haven't heard enough	Refused
All Respondents	21	18	14	46	2
Tea Party Supporters	85	1	9	4	–

80. Regardless of your overall opinion, do you think the views of the people involved in the Tea Party movement generally reflect the views of most Americans, or not?

	Reflect most Americans	Do not reflect most	Both/some (vol.)	DK/NA
All Respondents	25	36	2	38
Tea Party Supporters	84	8	3	4

81. How much difference do you think there is between the Republican Party and the Tea Party movement—a lot of difference, some difference, not much difference, or no difference at all?

	A lot	Some	Not much	None at all	DK/NA
All Respondents	11	29	18	8	34
Tea Party Supporters	19	61	13	4	3

82. Do you consider yourself to be a supporter of the Tea Party movement, or not?

	Yes	No	DK/NA
All Respondents	18	62	19

83. Is the Tea Party movement politically active in your community?

	Yes	No	DK/NA
All Respondents	21	51	28
Tea Party Supporters	50	40	10

84. Have you supported the Tea Party movement either by donating money or attending a rally or meeting, have you done both, or have you done neither?

	Donated money	Attended rally or meeting	Both	Neither	DK/NA
Tea Party Supporters	2	13	5	78	2

85. Have you visited Web sites associated with the Tea Party movement, or haven't you?

	Have	Have not	DK/NA
Tea Party Supporters	31	68	2

86. Where do you get most of your information about the Tea Party movement—1. the Internet, 2. email, 3. meetings, 4. phone calls, 5. television, 6. newspapers, or do you get your information from some other source?

	Tea Party Supporters
Internet	24
E-mail	4
Meetings	1
Phone calls	1
Television	47
Newspapers	8
Other source	11
DK/NA	3

87. Have you gotten or shared information about the Tea Party movement through Facebook, Twitter, or another social-networking site?

	Yes	No	DK/NA
Tea Party Supporters	11	88	2

88. Are you more likely to trust information you receive from other supporters of the Tea Party movement, or are you more likely to trust information you receive from television or newspapers?

	Other Supporters	Television/ newspapers	Both (vol.)	Neither (vol.)	DK/NA
Tea Party Supporters	45	37	5	7	6

89. What do you think should be the MAIN goal of the Tea Party movement—1. reducing the role of the federal government, 2. cutting the federal budget, 3. lowering taxes, 4. electing their own candidates, 5. creating jobs, or something else?

	Tea Party Supporters
Reduce federal government	45
Cutting budget	6
Lowering taxes	6
Electing own candidates	7
Creating jobs	9
Something else	7
All of them (vol.)	18
DK/NA	3

90. Have you ever been active in a political campaign—that is, have you worked for a candidate or party, contributed money, or done any other active work?

	Yes	No	DK/NA
Tea Party Supporters	43	56	1

91. Have you purchased gold coins or bars in the last twelve months, or not?

	Yes	No	DK/NA
Tea Party Supporters	5	93	3

[There are no questions 92 and 93.]

94. Think about past elections in which you have voted, including national and statewide elections. Would you say you always vote Republican, usually vote Republican, vote about equally for both parties, usually vote Democratic, or always vote Democratic?

	All Respondents	Tea Party Supporters
Always Republican	9	18
Usually Republican	19	48
Equally for both	31	25
Usually Democrat	16	3
Always Democrat	12	2
Never vote (vol.)	9	1
DK/NA	5	2

95. Which one of the following television networks do you watch most for information about politics and current events— ABC, CBS, NBC, CNN, Fox News Channel, MSNBC, or don't you watch television news?

	All Respondents	Tea Party Supporters
ABC, CBS, NBC	26	11
CNN	17	7
Fox News Channel	23	63
MSNBC	3	1
Don't watch news	16	6
Other	3	1
Combination (vol.)	11	10
DK/NA	1	1

96. Do you think of shows hosted by people like Glenn Beck and Sean Hannity more as news shows or more as entertainment?

	News	Entertainment	Both (vol.)	Neither (vol.)	DK/NA
All Respondents	24	44	5	4	23
Tea Party Supporters	53	25	11	2	8

97. How concerned are you that in the next twelve months you or someone else in your household might be out of work and looking for a job—very concerned, somewhat concerned, or not concerned at all?

	Very	Somewhat	Not at all	DK/NA
All Respondents	36	26	37	–
Tea Party Supporters	30	25	44	1

98. If you were asked to use one of these five names for your social class, which would you say you belong in—upper class, upper-middle class, middle class, working class, or lower class?

	Upper	Upper-middle	Middle	Working	Lower	DK/NA
All Respondents	2	10	40	34	13	1
Tea Party Supporters	3	15	50	26	5	2

99. Do you ever feel as if you're at risk of falling out of your current social class? (Based on those who named a class in question 98.)

	Yes	No	DK/NA
All Respondents	39	59	2
Tea Party Supporters	41	58	1

100. How would you rate the financial situation in your household these days? Is it very good, fairly good, fairly bad, or very bad?

	Very good	Fairly good	Fairly bad	Very bad	DK/NA
All Respondents	9	64	16	9	2
Tea Party Supporters	8	70	16	4	2

101. Which best describes the way you and your family have been affected by the recession? 1. The recession has been a hardship and caused major life changes; OR 2. The recession has been difficult but not caused any major life changes; OR 3. The recession has not had much effect one way or the other.

	Hardship	Difficult	Not much effect	DK/NA
All Respondents	19	50	30	–
Tea Party Supporters	14	55	30	1

102. Will someone in your household fill out the 2010 Census form and mail it back, or not?

	Will	Will not	Already did (vol.)	DK/NA
All Respondents	44	3	51	2
Tea Party Supporters	39	1	58	1

[There is no question 103.]

104. These last questions are for background only. Do you or does any other member of your household own a handgun, rifle, shotgun, or any other kind of firearm?

	Yes, self	Yes, other	Yes, self and other	No	DK/NA
All Respondents	21	13	7	56	3
Tea Party Supporters	31	12	15	32	10

105. Are you currently employed—either full-time or part-time—or are you temporarily out of work, or are you not in the market for work at all? IF NOT IN MARKET FOR WORK, ASK: Are you currently retired, or not?

	Currently employed	Temporarily out of work	Not in the market for work	Retired
All Respondents	54	15	13	18
Tea Party Supporters	56	6	5	32

106. Are you, or is any member of your immediate family, covered by Medicare?

	Yes, self	Yes, other	Yes, self and other	No	DK/NA
All Respondents	13	12	9	66	1
Tea Party Supporters	16	12	16	56	1

107. Are you, or is any member of your immediate family, currently receiving Social Security retirement benefits?

	Yes, self	Yes, other	Yes, self and other	No	DK/NA
All Respondents ·	12	12	8	67	1
Tea Party Supporters	17	13	18	51	–

Do you have any children? IF YES, ASK: Are any of your children under eighteen?

	Yes, under eighteen	Yes, over eighteen	No	DK/NA
All Respondents	34	33	33	–
Tea Party Supporters	20	53	26	1

108. Are your children currently enrolled in public school, or private school, or parochial school? (Based on parents of children under eighteen.)

	All Respondents	Tea Party Supporters
Public	70	65
Private	6	10
Parochial	2	5
Public & other	2	3
Homeschooled (vol.)	1	5
Not school age (vol.)	18	12
DK/NA	1	

Some people are registered to vote and others are not. Are you registered to vote in the precinct or election district where you now live, or aren't you?

	Yes	No
All Respondents	84	16
Tea Party Supporters	97	3

Would you say you attend religious services every week, almost every week, once or twice a month, a few times a year, or never?

	Every week	Almost every week	Once/ twice month	Few times a year	Never	DK/NA
All Respondents	27	8	12	26	25	1
Tea Party Supporters	38	12	11	22	16	1

Some people think of themselves as evangelical or born-again Christians. Do you ever think of yourself in either of these ways?

	Yes	No	DK/NA
All Respondents	28	70	2
Tea Party Supporters	39	58	2

What is your religious preference today?

	Protestant	Catholic	Jewish	Other	None	DK/NA
All Respondents	52	21	2	6	16	3
Tea Party Supporters	61	22	1	5	7	3

Are you now married, widowed, divorced, separated, or have you never been married?

	Married	Widowed	Divorced	Separated	Never married	DK/NA
All Respondents	52	8	12	1	27	–
Tea Party Supporters	70	7	9	1	11	1

Generally speaking, do you usually consider yourself a Republican, a Democrat, an Independent, or what?

	Republican	Democrat	Independent	DK/NA
All Respondents	28	31	33	7
Tea Party Supporters	54	5	36	5

How would you describe your views on most political matters? Generally do you think of yourself as liberal, moderate, or conservative? IF LIBERAL, ASK: Would you say you are very liberal or only somewhat liberal? IF CONSERVATIVE, ASK: Would you say you are very conservative or only somewhat conservative?

	Very liberal	Some-what liberal	Moderate	Some-what conser-vative	Very conser-vative	DK/NA
All Respondents	4	16	38	22	12	8
Tea Party Supporters	–	4	20	34	39	3

How old are you?

	18–29	30–44	45–64	Over 64	Refused
All Respondents	23	27	34	16	1
Tea Party Supporters	7	16	46	29	1

What was the last grade in school you completed?

	Not a high school graduate	High school graduate	Some college	College graduate	Post-graduate work
All Respondents	12	35	28	15	10
Tea Party Supporters	3	26	33	23	14

Are you of Hispanic origin or descent, or not?

	Hispanic	Not Hispanic	DK/NA
All Respondents	12	87	1
Tea Party Supporters	3	95	1

Are you white, black, Asian, or some other race?

	White	Black	Asian	Other	Refused
All Respondents	77	12	3	7	2
Tea Party Supporters	89	1	1	6	3

Was your total family income in 2008 UNDER or OVER $50,000? IF UNDER, ASK: Was it under $15,000, between $15,000 and $30,000, or between $30,000 and $50,000? IF OVER, ASK: Was it between $50,000 and $75,000, or between $75,000 and $100,000, or was it over $100,000?

	Under $15,000	$15,000–$29,999	$30,000–$49,999	$50,000–$74,999	$75,000–$100,000	Over $100,000	Refused
All Respondents	10	22	16	18	12	14	7
Tea Party Supporters	5	13	17	25	11	20	9

Was it over $250,000, or not?

	Yes, over $250,000	No	DK/NA
All Respondents	11	83	6
Tea Party Supporters	12	87	1

	Male	Female
All Respondents	49	51
Tea Party Supporters	59	41

Acknowledgments

Writing a book would be one thing. Writing a book about an unfolding story, on an unforgiving deadline, is another. I owe many people thanks for making it easier.

Above all, I thank the people whose stories are chronicled in this book, who allowed me to trail them around and answered endless questions over a period of months. In particular: Jennifer Turner Stefano, Diana Reimer, Keli Carender, Tom Grimes, Anastasia Przybylski, Brendan Steinhauser, and Adam Brandon.

The following works (and in many cases, their authors, who made themselves available for interviews) provided essential reading: Michael Kazin's *The Populist Persuasion*, Lisa McGirr's *Suburban Warriors*, Donald I. Warren's *The Radical Center*, Sam Tanenhaus's *The Death of Conservatism*, Bruce Schulman's *The Seventies*, and Mark Lilla's "The Tea Party Jacobins" in the *New York Review of Books*. Thanks as well to Randy Barnett of Georgetown University Law Center and Andrew Kohut of the Pew Research Center for helping me understand the legal and political backdrop of the Tea Party. And I am grateful to

Michelle Bowker White for allowing me to quote extensively from her mother's letter in chapter three.

This book started with stories I wrote for the *New York Times*, so the list of thanks there is long. Enormous thanks to Suzanne Daley, who had the idea that conservatives might be interesting to cover in 2009, and to Rick Berke, who with Suzanne shaped early stories and instantly and enthusiastically embraced the idea that I should write this book. Suzanne and Rick then swiftly convinced Bill Keller, Jill Abramson, and Bill Schmidt of the same thing, and I thank them, as well, for their support.

At the *Week in Review*, Dave Smith, Mary Suh, and the incomparable Mary Jo Murphy pushed me to ask more and better questions. In the Washington bureau, Dick Stevenson provided his ever-wise counsel on stories. Katy Roberts provided phone numbers and thoughts and made the Room for Debate blog a provocative crib sheet for thinking about the Tea Party.

In the polling department, I thank Janet Elder, Megan Thee-Brenan, Marjorie Connelly, and Dalia Sussman for designing the groundbreaking poll that the paper published in April 2010, and for breaking out data for this book, and Marina Stefan for conducting the follow-up interviews.

Ben Werschkul caught more with his video camera than I ever could with my eye, and his observations and determination to the get the story from all angles helped push me to get more, too. Steve Crowley and Jim Wilson not only captured the movement in terrific images, they were insightful and game travel partners.

I thank Alex Ward for his thoughtful edits and help on various practical issues, and Phyllis Collazo for digging through photo archives. Alix Pelletier Paul, as always, made the logistics seem more logical.

Many friends and colleagues helped, as constructive readers, or by offering sources, explanations, perspective or support of one kind and another at critical moments. I am grateful to them all: Carolyn Ryan, Adam Liptak, Ginia Bellafante, Randy Kennedy, Monica Davey, Jim Rutenberg, Jeff Zeleny, Carl Hulse, Jackie Calmes, Danielle Mattoon, Alison Mitchell, Kit Seelye, Adam Nagourney, Leslie Kaufman, Tim O'Brien, and David Kirkpatrick.

At Times Books/Henry Holt, my great thanks go to Paul Golob, the most energetic and engaged of editors. His thoroughness, not to mention his organizational skills, was everything a writer could hope for. I also thank John Sterling, who first came up with the idea for this book. Emi Ikkanda helped with photos, permissions, and other tasks that saved me valuable time. My agent, Elyse Cheney, hard-nosed and big-hearted, made me feel in good hands the whole way.

To other friends, deep thanks: Ben Sherwood for not being above the news, Sarah and San Orr for their abiding support and eagle eyes, Susan Pasternak for cheerleading, Jessica Yellin for updates from the field, and my old partner in crime, Scot Lehigh, for careful edits. I would have been lost without Daryl Levinson, who read, reread, and advised—Sarah Palin says we don't need a constitutional law professor, but I did.

Thanks to Marcia Marley and Peter Rappoport, Per Lofving and Martha Evans, and Thad Hayes and Adam Lippin for being the village. And to the unflappable Nora Coote for making it possible for me to travel knowing my children are in loving and steady hands, and for her resourcefulness in finding diversions that allowed me quiet to write.

This book is dedicated to my parents, Frits and Barbara Backus Zernike, for raising their children to view—and appreciate—this ever-amazing country with the freshness of a foreigner's eye. Their public spirit inspires me, their sense of humor has sustained me. The stories my father told us around the dinner table were my first and remain my favorite. He has believed in a book before there was even a book idea. When I was about five years old, my mother gave me a book called *Mommies at Work* that had been published, remarkably ahead of its time, in 1955. I did not cotton to the concept, but it is proof of my mother's great grace that she has forgotten all that, or at least pretended to, and has done everything she can to make it possible for me to be among what the book (above a picture of a typewriter) calls the Writer Mommies.

My brothers, Frits and Harry, and my sister-in-law, Jennifer Wu, have been tireless supporters, advocates, readers, and editors (photo, word, and otherwise). And my children, Frits and Nico, are the world's best incentive to get off deadline. (Yes, Frits, I am finished.)

But my biggest thanks are to my husband, Jonathan Schwartz, who goes off to do his bit to cure cancer every day yet still believes in the power of a little cause like journalism to change the world. He talked through ideas, read background articles and got as excited about them as I did, edited drafts, plus made sure the family ate regular meals. The song still says it best: *And it's you*. And I cannot thank you enough.

Index

abortion, 4, 7, 14, 37, 58, 62, 63, 70, 87, 103, 111, 143, 192, 214, 220, 230, 231, 233

Ackerman, Peter, 38

Adams, David, 168–70, 179, 187

Adams, Samuel, 34–35, 83

AFL-CIO, 36

AIG, 27, 28

Alinsky, Saul, 3, 38, 42, 45, 54, 83

America: Freedom to Fascism (film), 166

American Conservative Union, 156

Americans for Legal Immigration PAC, 189

Americans for Tax Reform, 156

American Spectator, The, 22

Americans with Disabilities Act, 179

Anderson, Frank, 143

Anger Is Brewing, 155

Angle, Sharron, 150, 154, 186–87, 195

AngryRenter.com, 36

anti-Communism, 54, 57, 74

Anti-Porkulus Protest (Seattle), 18–19

Arguing with Idiots (Beck), 77

Arizona immigration law, 190–91

Arizona Republican U.S. Senate primary, 5, 106

Armey, Dick, 34–37, 43–45, 47, 67, 76, 87, 126, 138, 157, 159, 163, 189, 193

Armey's Axioms, 35, 39, 193

As a Mom, 109, 149

Ashjian, Scott, 154–55

Aspen Institute, 160

Astroturf, 4, 88, 125, 156

Atlas Shrugged (Rand), 14, 26

Austrian economic school, 2, 37–38, 164–65, 177

auto companies, 6, 16, 29, 77, 136, 144, 172

Bachmann, Michele, 1, 201, 205, 209, 223

bailouts, 6–7, 16, 28–29, 59, 169, 172

balanced budget amendment, 170, 175

banks and financial industry, 6, 10, 27, 28, 38, 66, 70, 76, 147, 150, 152, 181

Barton, Joe, 188

Bastiat, Frederic, 38, 77, 128, 157, 165

Beck, Glenn, 4–5, 23–25, 46, 74–75, 77, 85, 87, 109, 138, 149, 151, 169, 188, 223–24, 237

Beckstrom, Rod A., 38

Bennett, Robert, 104

BigGovernment.com, 126

bloggers, 40, 41

Bluegrass Institute, 168

Boehner, John, 138, 200, 209, 223

Boston Globe, The, 90

Boston Red Sox, 90

Boston Tea Party, 34, 52–53, 167

Bowker, Anne, 49–50, 52

Boxer, Barbara, 94

BP oil spill, 187–88

Brafman, Ori, 38

Brandon, Adam, 36–37, 40–41

Brown, Scott, 81–82, 86, 88–92, 97, 120, 122, 155–56, 162, 186, 209, 223

Buckley, William F., Jr., 128, 166

Bucks County, Pennsylvania, Republican Party, 109–10
  executive committee, 109–10
  local committee, 101–2, 107, 109–11, 114–19, 183–86
  state representative elections, 114, 117–18, 185

Bucks County Tea Party, 29, 66, 101–2, 109–19
  Washington Crossing Historic Park rally, 29, 31–32, 66, 108–9

Bunning, Jim, 161, 164, 168, 176

Bush, George H. W., 223

Bush, George W., 15–16, 31, 51, 103, 108, 218, 222–23

Cain, Herman, 205

California Republican U.S. Senate primary, 186

Callaham, Kelly, 173

Campaign for Liberty, 26, 165, 169

Cantwell, Maria, 16

cap-and-trade policy, 37, 82, 89, 103, 115, 158

carbon tax, 35

"card check." See Employee Free Choice Act

Carender, Keli, 13–19, 62, 84, 128–31, 135, 191, 195

Carter, Jimmy, 137, 223

Carville, James, 126, 153

Castle, Michael N., 197

Cato Institute, 18, 35

Cavuto, Neil, 23

charity, 62, 74, 75, 128–29

Cheney, Dick, 176

Chilberg, Susan, 65

China, 108

Christian conservatives, 105

Church, Jeff, 147

church and state, separation of, 75

Citizens for a Sound Economy (later FreedomWorks), 35

Civil Rights Act (1964), 57, 178–79

civil rights movement, 55, 138–39

Civil War, 72

Clark County (Nevada) Republican Committee, 106–7

Cleaver, Emanuel, 138

Clemente, Matt, 89

Clinton, Bill, 16, 35, 103, 126, 223

Clinton, Hillary, 28–29, 223

Close, Dee, 152

CNBC, 13

CNN, 16

Coakley, Martha, 82, 90–91, 155

coal mining, 158, 173, 176

Code Pink, 157

college loans and subsidies, 181
Collins, Susan, 208
Colorado Republican primary, 5
commerce clause, 71–72
Common Sense (Beck), 77
"Communist in the White
    House, A" (song), 1, 158
Communism, 2, 36, 75
Congressional Budget Office, 10,
    147
Conscience of a Conservative, The
    (Goldwater), 56
Conservative Leadership Coalition,
    100, 118
Continental Congress, Second, 66
Contract from America, 67,
    143–44, 200
Contract with America, 45
Conway, Jack, 179, 187
Cosmopolitan magazine, 88
Coulter, Ann, 156
Council on Foreign Relations, 74
Countrywide Financial, 36
credit card companies, 144
Crist, Charlie, 19–20, 40, 86,
    104–5, 162
Cuomo, Andrew, 203

DailyPaul (website), 168
Daschle, Tom, 34
Davey, Nancy, 148
Davies, Mariann, 29–30
Day, Wendy, 144
Dean, Howard, 47, 105
"death panels," 83
debt ceiling, 201, 204, 209
Declaration of Independence, 79
Dedication and Leadership (Hyde),
    2, 38
Defense of Marriage Act, 192
defense spending, 44, 151, 158
Demers, Andrew, 177
democracy, republic vs., 75
Democracy Corps, 153

Democratic National Committee,
    47
Democratic Party, 28–29, 36, 43,
    83–85, 109, 114–15, 192
    primaries and caucuses of 2004
        and 2008, 105
"democratic socialism," 77
Denver, Colorado, protests 19
Derry, Chris, 168
DeVore, Chuck, 186
Dicks, Norm, 84
Dodd, Christopher, 36
Dooley, Debbie, 87
Drudge Report, 126
Duncan, Mike, 173
Duvall, Jack, 38

economic insecurity, 58–60, 164.
    See also Great Recession
economic policy, 7, 38, 72, 76, 78,
    165
economic stimulus, 7, 10, 16,
    18–20, 23, 29, 40, 65, 86–87
education, 38, 69, 72, 131–32, 150
Education, Department of, 77, 180
Edwards, Mickey, 59, 60
elections, 101. *See also specific states*
    of 1980, 137
    of 1992, 60, 103, 147
    of 1994, 192
    of 1996, 103
    of 2000, 60, 192
    of 2004, 60
    of 2006, 109, 195
    of 2008, 8, 16, 26, 28–31, 60,
        107–9, 154–55, 163–64, 167,
        195
    of 2010, 5, 36, 79, 104, 106,
        186, 192, 193, 195–99
    of 2012, 95
Emanuel, Rahm, 151
Employee Free Choice Act ("card
    check"), 36, 37, 87, 89
Endangered Species Act, 144

Energy, Department of, 179
Ensign, John, 147
Environmental Protection Agency,
173

Facebook, 11, 22, 40, 61
Farah, Joseph, 95–96, 189
federal budget deficits, 10, 16,
31, 51, 103, 151, 176, 180,
191–92
federal government, powers of,
68–73, 76–77
Federalist Papers, The, 77, 104
Federal Reserve, 38, 69, 115, 151,
166, 181, 225
Federation for American
Immigration Reform, 190
Feingold, Russell, 198
Fifteenth Amendment, 72
fifty-state strategy, 47
Filburn, Roscoe, 71–72
Fiorina, Carly, 186
first principles, 79
fiscal responsibility, 43, 111, 135,
143, 180, 192. *See also* federal
budget deficits
Fitzpatrick, Mike, 110–14
5000 Year Leap, The (Skousen),
74–75, 78, 167
Fletcher, Tom, 173
Florida Republican U.S. Senate
primary, 19, 86, 104,
162–63
food safety laws, 172
Force More Powerful, A (Ackerman
and Duvall), 38, 46
Ford, Gerald, 66
Founding Fathers, 8, 21, 47, 67,
73–75, 94, 104, 165, 167, 170
Fourteenth Amendment, 72
Fox News, 4–5, 10, 23, 61, 109,
132, 142
Francis, Don, 146–47
Francis, Shirl, 146–47

Frank, Barney, 100–101, 138
Franklin, Benjamin, 21
FreedomWorks, 4, 33–38, 42–43,
45–47, 120–21, 125, 134,
138, 188, 191–92, 196
Facebook page, 40
founding of, 35–38
Liberty Summit, 156
Massachusetts U.S. Senate
election and, 88–90
New York Twenty-third District
election and, 86
9/12 marches and, 85, 89, 188
Tax Day rallies and, 1–2, 156–58
free markets, 24, 38, 43, 152, 168,
190
Freire, J. P., 22
Friedman, Milton, 60, 128

Gadsden, Christopher, 66
gas prices, 29, 51
gay marriage, 7, 15, 42, 58, 59, 60,
62, 87, 103, 143, 163, 192,
231
gay rights, 101
George Mason University protests,
136–37
Gheen, William, 189
Gibbs, Robert, 21
Gilbert, Richard, 152
Gingrich, Newt, 223
*Give Us Liberty: A Tea Party
Manifesto* (Armey and Kibbe),
189
Gladwell, Malcolm, 2, 38
Glass, Philip, 105–6
global warming, 35, 58, 112,
157–58
Glover, Bob, 145
Goldwater, Barry, 6, 45, 52, 54–56,
59, 178, 193
Google, 41–43, 95
Gorbachev, Mikhail, 36
Gore, Al, 60, 158

Gotkis, Steve, 116–18
government shutdown, 201
Graham, Lindsey, 82, 179, 189–90
grassroots, 4–6, 33, 54–56, 123
Grateful Dead, 36, 125
Grayson, Charles Merwin "Trey,"
    III, 160–63, 169, 172–77,
    206
Great Depression, 73, 78, 180–81
Great Recession (economic collapse
    of 2008 and aftermath), 6, 11,
    16–17, 53, 60, 78, 147, 150,
    167, 168, 180
Great Society, 143
Greenberg, Stanley, 153
Grimes, Tom, 11, 65, 77–79,
    127–28, 189

Hamilton, Alexander, 76
Hancock, John, 34
Hannity, Sean, 23, 237
Harper, Gil, 93
Harper, Susan, 93
Harris, Richard, 152
Harrisburg, Pennsylvania, march,
    133
Hatch, Orrin, 204
Hayek, Friedrich, 38, 142, 178,
    189
Hayworth, J. D., 106
health care reform, 6, 8, 10, 27,
    53, 59, 62, 66, 67, 69, 82–84,
    89, 91, 103–4, 112–13, 120,
    125–29, 135–41, 145–50,
    169, 180, 187, 192
  attempt of 1940s, 52
  attempt of 1993, 35, 83
  Paul Ryan and, 201–2
health savings accounts, 62, 113
Hecker, Ryan, 67
Hochul, Kathy, 208
Hoffman, Doug, 87, 163
Hoffman, Ira, 112–13
homeschooling, 62, 163, 172

Housing and Urban Development,
    Department of, 77
Houston Tea Party Society, 67
Huckabee, Mike, 223
Hyde, Douglas, 2, 38

IAmWithRick.com, 40
immigration, 16, 29, 58, 60, 65,
    95, 107, 112, 149, 189, 214,
    215, 220, 230
Independence Caucus, 69–70, 104,
    143
Independence Day rallies, 85, 133
individualism, 10, 61–62, 125
inflation, 57
infrastructure spending, 38
Internal Revenue Service, 166
Iraq War, 176

Jackson, Victoria, 158, 159
Jamestown settlement, 75–76
Jefferson, Thomas, 21, 30, 45, 66,
    75, 124, 128
Jim Crow South, 72
jobs, 10, 89, 172
John Birch Society, 55–57, 74, 85,
    166
Johnson, Jim, 177
Johnson, Lyndon B., 51, 173
Johnson, Ron, 197

Kaine, Tim, 93
Katrina, Hurricane, 167
Kazin, Michael, 53–54
Kelly, Basil, 149–50
Kelly, Kathryn, 149–50
Kelly, Kevin, 121
Kennedy, Edward "Ted," 82, 88–91
Kennedy, John F., 55
Kentucky Republican U.S. Senate
    primary, 5, 160–63, 167–78
Kentucky Taxpayers United, 167
Kerry, John, 60
Keynesian economics, 78

Kibbe, Matt, 34–35, 37–38,
   46–47, 88–89, 125, 157, 159,
   189, 192
King, Martin Luther, Jr., 2, 85
King, Steve, 121, 157
Kinnison, Barbee, 94
Koch family, 35
Kyl, Jon, 178

labor unions, 9, 37, 87, 125
Landis, Debbie, 155–56
LaRouche, Lyndon, 125–26
Las Vegas, Nevada, Republican
   Party, 106–7
Las Vegas Review-Journal, 155
Law, The (Bastiat), 38, 77, 157, 165
Leahy, Michael Patrick, 21–22, 26,
   84
Lefner, Kim, 148
Levin, Mark, 77, 141
Lewis, John, 138–39
Lexington, Kentucky, Tea Party
   Rally, 168
libertarians, 7–9, 15, 19, 26, 37, 52,
   57, 112, 143, 154, 162–65,
   168, 171, 177, 193, 202
Liberty and Tyranny (Levin), 77
Liberty Belle blog, 17, 191
Lilla, Mark, 61, 62
Limbaugh, Rush, 18
Lincoln, Blanche, 193
Lingenfelter, Tom, 113
lobbying, 42, 101, 120–21
Louisville, Kentucky, Tea Party,
   172
Lowden, Sue, 154, 186
Lugar, Richard, 204–5
"Lump Reports," 154
Luntz, Frank, 109

Madison, James, 104
"Making of America, The"
   (seminar), 65
Malkin, Michelle, 18, 19

March on Washington of 1963, 2,
   46. *See also* Washington, D.C.,
   rallies
Maricopa County, Arizona,
   Republican committee, 106
Martin, Jenny Beth, 25–26, 43,
   84–85, 88, 96–97, 109, 121,
   192, 205, 206
Mason, George, 76
Massachusetts
   state health reform, 91
   U.S. Senate special election of
      2010, 81–82, 86–92, 122,
      155, 162
McCain, John, 8, 28, 31, 107–8,
   154, 186, 223
McCarthy, Joseph, 54–55, 166
McConnell, Mitch, 161, 173,
   175–79, 187
McGirr, Lisa, 54–55
McHugh, John, 86
McKenzie, Martha, 152–53
McNassar, Conor, 14, 17
McQueen, Jeff, 81–82, 144, 157
Media Matters for America, 142
Medicaid, 74, 77, 167
Medicare, 9, 15, 28, 63, 74, 77,
   78, 103, 135–37, 142, 151,
   167, 180, 187, 193, 207,
   208, 229, 241
Medved, Michael, 18
Meet the Press (TV show), 179
Michiana 9/12, 65, 74
"Middle American Radicals," 50,
   57–58
Miller, Joe, 197
minimum wage, 70, 71
Minutemen, 66
Mises, Ludwig von, 38, 142, 178
Monckton, Lord, 157–59
Mormons, 74
mortgage crisis, 6, 13, 16, 20, 23,
   27, 132, 181
MoveOn.org, 31, 37, 108, 192

MSNBC, 178
Murkowski, Frank, 197
Murkowski, Lisa, 197, 208
Murphy, Patrick, 43, 109–10
Murray, Patty, 16

National Center for Constitutional
    Studies, 65, 74, 167
national debt, 6, 16, 19, 31, 42, 51,
    100, 108, 111, 162, 180, 193
National Institutes of Health, 77
National Precinct Alliance, 105–6
National Republican Senatorial
    Committee, 86, 187
National Review, 15
national security, 100, 165
National Tea Party Convention
    (Nashville, February 2010),
    92–98, 128, 142–43
National Tea Party Unity
    Convention (Las Vegas,
    October 2010), 188
Natural Law, 74
Nelson, Ben, 91
Network (film), 24
Nevada Republican U.S. Senate
    primary, 5, 106–7, 154–56, 186
New Deal, 55, 70–72, 78, 113,
    143, 180
New Hampshire primary, 177
news media, 9, 10, 40, 126
New York Review of Books, 61
New York Times/CBS News poll
    (April 2010), 6, 9, 10, 51, 53,
    57, 58, 126, 150, 211–43
New York Twenty-third
    Congressional District special
    election (2009), 86–87, 105,
    126, 162
"9/12 Project, The," 5, 24–26, 43,
    46, 65, 73–74, 79, 85, 89, 109,
    128, 134, 159, 169, 188, 194
    Washington, D.C., rallies, 46, 50,
    85–86, 89, 128, 134, 188, 194

Ning, 26, 46, 61
NumbersUSA, 190

Oath Keepers, 85, 148, 187
Obama, Barack, 1, 4, 13, 20, 24,
    28, 40, 42, 53, 58, 65, 78, 85,
    95, 112, 125, 136, 147–48,
    150, 151, 157, 176, 185, 189,
    195
    accusations about birth certificate
    of, 51, 95–96
    BP oil spill and, 188
    election of 2008 and, 5, 8, 10,
    16, 19, 22, 31, 39, 47, 59–60,
    105, 107–8, 118, 135
    inauguration of, 83
    New York Times/CBS News
    poll and, 213–14, 216–18,
    222–23, 226–28
Odom, Eric, 26, 92
O'Donnell, Christine, 196–97
oil, 108, 112
Oljar, Sally, 129
Olympia, Washington, rally, 128
One World Order, 74
Organizing for America, 10–11
originalism, 7–8, 38, 68–72, 75,
    104, 144, 167

Paine, Thomas, 66, 171
Palin, Sarah, 22, 39, 83, 93, 97–98,
    147, 156, 163, 177, 197, 206,
    223, 225
Pappas, Max, 36
Parson, Bill, 154
Patriot Act, 176
*Patriot's History of the United
    States, A*, 78
Paul, Kelley, 167, 172
Paul, Randal "Rand," 56, 67,
    161–64, 167–81, 183,
    186–88, 194, 195, 197, 199,
    205, 206, 208
Paul, Robert, 171

Paul, Ron, 2, 19, 26, 56, 65, 151, 154–55, 158, 162–65, 177–78, 223–24
Paul Forums (website), 168
Pawlenty, Tim, 206
Pelosi, Nancy, 3, 95
Pennsylvania Republican Party committee elections, 183–85 primaries, 5, 86
People's Party, 54
Perkins, Frances, 71
Perot, Ross, 53, 60, 103, 147
Perry, Rick, 223
Pew Research Center, 9, 60
Phillips, Judson, 92–94, 96–98
Pike, Cliff, 171–72
Pike, Nancy, 171
Poprik, Pat, 109–10, 113–14, 185
populism, 53–54, 57, 61, 70, 73
Populist Persuasion, The (Kazin), 53–54
Przybylski, Anastasia, 28–30, 42–43, 109–12
public choice theory, 37–38

Quinn, Sheri, 164–65, 167, 169
Quinn, Tim, 164–65

race and racism, 4–5, 51–52, 55–60, 62, 72, 107, 108, 138–39, 166, 178–80, 213, 227, 232, 243
Rachel Maddow Show, The (TV show), 178
Radical Center, The (Warren), 57
Radio France, 93
Raffle, Andy, 118–20
Rakovich, Mary, 19–20, 23, 40
Rand, Ayn, 14, 26, 128, 162
Randolph, A. Philip, 46
Reagan, Ronald, 55, 78–79, 97, 137, 166–67, 181
Real George Washington, The (Parry and Allison), 166

Reform Party, 53, 103
Reid, Harry, 94, 106, 146–50, 154–55, 187, 195
Reimer, Diana, 27, 91, 120–25, 127, 132–38, 140–41, 190–91
Reimer, Don, 27, 123, 132–35, 137, 140, 190
Renshaw, Ryan, 166–67, 170
Repisky, Bernadette, 115
Republican National Committee, 38, 93, 97, 102, 161, 173
Republican National Convention (2008), 22
Republican Party, 4–5, 8, 46. See also specific state and local parties
Armey as ambassador to, 43
conservative insurgencies in, 6
local committee candidate endorsements, 109–11, 113–14
local committee elections, 101–2, 105–19, 183–86
local precinct elections, 101–2, 105–6
presidential nomination campaign of 2008 and, 19, 107
primaries and, 5, 86, 104, 106, 186
Tea Party distrust of, 5, 31, 82–83, 85–88, 97–98, 150–51, 203–5
Tea Party influence on, 191, 195, 206, 209
Tea Party takeover attempts and, 100–119
Republican Revolution of 1994, 103, 118, 195
Reveille for Radicals (Alinsky), 39
Revolutionary War, 53, 66, 149
right-wing extremism, 85, 166
RINOs (Republicans in Name Only), 103

Road to Serfdom, The (Hayek), 189
Roberts, Owen J., 71
Roddy, John, 150
Roddy, Shirley, 150
Roe v. Wade, 58, 112, 233
Romney, Mitt, 22, 177, 223
Roosevelt, Franklin D., 36, 70–71, 73, 78
Ross, Betsy, 81
Rubio, Marco, 86, 162–63
Rules for Radicals (Alinsky), 3, 38–39
Russo, Aaron, 166
Rustin, Bayard, 2, 46
Ryan, Paul, 201
  budget, 208

Sam Adams Alliance, 124–25
Santelli, Rick, 13, 20–24, 26–27, 29, 40, 115, 177, 181
Saudi Arabia, 108
Scalia, Antonin, 68
Schilling, Curt, 90
school board elections, 105, 115
school busing, 51, 52, 59
Schulman, Bruce, 57, 61
Scozzafava, Dede, 86–87, 105, 163
Searchlight, Nevada, Tea Party, 145–50, 155–56
Seattle Sons and Daughters of Liberty, 19, 129
Second Amendment, 70
Second American Revolution, 104
  flag, 81, 156
September 11, 2001, attacks, 5, 134, 176
Seventeenth Amendment, 70
Seventies, The (Schulman), 57
Shreeve, Anthony, 96
Sixteenth Amendment, 69, 166
Skoda, Mark, 92–95
Skousen, W. Cleon, 73–75, 167
slavery, 76

small business, 10, 131
Snowe, Olympia, 203, 208
socialism, 75, 78, 84
social issues, 42, 70, 95, 143, 189, 191
social networking, 22, 26, 60
Social Security, 9, 28, 36–37, 57, 63, 69–73, 78, 136–37, 151, 164, 180, 187, 193, 198, 229, 241
Sons of Liberty, 34
South Carolina, 23, 135
Sowell, Thomas, 15, 128
Specter, Arlen, 84, 86, 133, 193
Stallard, Joan, 157
Starfish and the Spider, The (Brafman and Beckstrom), 38
state budget cuts, 129, 131–32
StateBudgetSolutions.Org, 191
state sovereignty, 67
states' rights, 68–70, 77
Steele, Michael, 93, 97
Stefano, Jennifer Turner, 30–32, 99–105, 107–9, 113–19, 139, 183–85, 192
Steinhauser, Brendan, 2–4, 38–43, 45–48, 88–89, 121, 125, 138, 157, 189, 193–94
Stivers, Steve, 198
Stone, Harlan Fiske, 71
Suburban Warriors (McGirr), 54–55
Sunshine Review, 191
Suntato, Kathy, 115
supervoters, 102

Taft, Robert, 55
Tancredo, Tom, 95
Tarkanian, Danny, 150, 154, 186
Tarkanian, Jerry, 150
Tax Day rallies, 2–5, 23, 26, 30, 33, 42, 46, 52, 66–67, 100–101, 132–33, 156–57
Tax Day Tea Party website, 26

taxes, 65, 104, 112, 115, 118, 151,
    181
  federal progressive income, 38,
    54, 69, 76, 165, 181
  flat, 35, 37
  health care and, 129
  small business and, 130–31
  state, 129–31, 203
tax revolts of 1970s, 52, 57
Taylor, Jared, 64, 73, 75–77,
    79–80
Tea Party. *See also* Tax Day rallies;
    and specific conventions, local
    groups, and protests
  2010 elections and, 195–99
  action kit, 189
  activists vs. supporters, 7,
    150–52, 199–200
  Angle primary win in Nevada
    and, 186–87
  beginning and early growth of, 4,
    13–32, 83–85
  Brown win in Massachusetts and,
    81–83, 86–92
  budget cut proposals, 200–201
  Constitution and, 64–80
  distrust of big government and,
    6, 9, 43, 61–63, 150–53,
    166–67, 187–88, 193, 200
  divisions in, and goals of, 8–9,
    11, 60, 96–97, 142–46,
    150–55, 189
  early precursors of, 50–61
  flags of, 1, 81–82, 86, 144, 147,
    155–56, 188
  FreedomWorks support for,
    33–48, 155–56, 189
  ideology and, 7, 42, 112,
    128–29, 135–36, 192–93,
    200, 205, 207
  impact of, 186–93, 195–99
  local Republican parties and,
    99–119, 183–86
  Nevada ballot line and, 154
  passion, mission, and community
    and, 11, 37, 39, 122–35, 148
  presidential candidates for 2012,
    205–6
  profile of, 4, 6–11, 211–23
  Rand Paul primary win in
    Kentucky and, 160–77, 187–88
  structure of, 189–90
  women as organizers of, 109
Tea Party Express, 84–85, 90,
    145–46, 148, 155–56, 197
Tea Party Nation, 92, 96, 190
Tea Party Patriots, 26, 43, 84, 87,
    96–97, 109, 120–21, 126–27,
    129, 132–34, 139, 143, 159,
    190–92, 205
Tea Party: The Documentary Film
    (film), 88
Tenth Amendment, 69, 97, 104,
    112–13
Tessler, Ben, 121
textbook wars, 52, 59, 80
Thirteenth Amendment, 72
Thomas, Clarence, 68
Thomas Jefferson Club, 32, 100,
    115
Tipping Point, The (Gladwell), 2, 38
Toomey, Pat, 86, 197
Top Conservatives, 22
Tricare, 28, 135
Troubled Asset Relief Program
    (TARP), 16, 28, 29
Twitter, 22, 26, 61, 177

unemployment, 65, 78, 107, 144,
    176
University of Chicago Press, 189
U.S. Chamber of Commerce, 38
U.S. Congress, 5, 7, 34, 53, 67,
    83–84, 97, 103, 135–39, 167,
    170, 179–80, 216–18, 222
  elections of 2010 and, 192–93,
    195–97
  powers of, 68–72, 76–78

U.S. Constitution, 7–8, 38, 47, 55, 56, 64–80, 84, 104, 123, 144, 148–49, 151–53, 164, 167, 180, 189, 192
U.S. House of Representatives, 126, 137–39, 145
U.S. Senate, 34, 145. *See also specific state primaries*
    Brown win in Massachusetts and, 88–92
    direct election and, 70
    Energy Committee, 173
U.S. Supreme Court, 68, 70–72
U.S. Tea Party website, 33–34
Utah Republican U.S. Senate primary, 104, 162

Venezuela, 108
Vietnam War, 58
Virginia, Fifth District, 154
Voight, Jon, 140
Vorin, Bob, 88

Walker, Scott, 203
Walsh, Joe, 198–99
Warner, Melinda, 142–43
war on terror, 176
Warren, Donald, 49–51, 57, 59
Warren, Tony, 52, 106
Washington, George, 29, 66, 73
Washington, D.C., rallies. *See also* March on Washington of 1963
    February 2009, 45–47

September 2009, "9/12," 46, 50, 85–86, 89, 128, 134
November 2009, health care, 127
March 2010, health care, 120–24, 137–41
April 2010, Tax Day, 1–5, 156–59
August 2010, 188
September 2010, 188, 194
Washington state legislature, 129–31
welfare, 38, 58
West, Allen, 198
West Virginia textbook protests of 1970s, 59
White, Jodine, 9
Wickard v. Filburn, 71, 104
Wilbur, Kirby, 18, 128
Williams, Mark, 155
Wisconsin, clash over collective bargaining rights, 203
Wolbe, Donna, 181
Wood, Gordon, 53
Worcester Tea Party, 89
WorldNetDaily, 95, 189
Wright, Jeremiah, 176
Wyzanski, Charles, Jr., 72–73

Young Professionals for Bush, 161
Young Republicans, 15, 131
YouTube, 4, 21, 22, 61, 84

About the Author

KATE ZERNIKE is a national correspondent for the *New York Times* and was a member of the team that shared the 2002 Pulitzer Prize for explanatory reporting. She has covered education, Congress, and four national elections for the *Times* and was previously a reporter for the *Boston Globe*. She lives with her family outside New York City.